Keto Diet Book UK

Simple and Healthy Keto Diet Recipes Easy to Follow and Good for Your Health

ISBN: 9798697182888

TABLE OF CONTENTS

LUNCH RECIPE 39

"Since the 1960s, different variations of ketogenic diets have also become widely known as weight-loss methods," she says, and for some Americans, it's become their go-to way to control their weight. This might be a good option for some people, Leman says, because "the emphasis on 'whole foods' such as fish and seafood, low-carb vegetables, nuts, seeds and berries as the foundation of a keto diet is certainly healthier than the calorie-dense, nutrient-poor, refined, processed foods that form the foundation of the standard American diet.

Daryl Gioffre, celebrity nutritionist and author of "Get Off Your Acid," says that "anything is a good alternative to the standard American diet. The SAD diet is an extremely acidic diet that's pumped up with inflammatory foods, fats, and sugars. It's wreaking havoc on peoples' health." The ketogenic diet – when done correctly – can be a great alternative.

What is Keto Diet?

The keto diet emphasizes weight loss through fat-burning. The goal is to quickly lose weight and ultimately feel fuller with fewer cravings while boosting your mood, mental focus, and energy. According to Keto proponents, by slashing the carbs you consume and instead filling up on fats, you safely enter a state of ketosis. That's when the body breaks down both dietary and stored body fat into substances called ketones. Your fat-burning system now relies mainly on fat – instead of sugar – for energy. While similar in some ways to familiar low-carb diets, the keto diet's extreme carb restrictions – about 20 net carbs a day or less, depending on the version – and the deliberate shift into ketosis are what set this increasingly popular diet apart. Other eating plans are pulling in keto elements, so you can find versions like eco-keto and at least one commercial diet that incorporates keto-friendly products.

The keto diet has its roots in the decades-old therapeutic ketogenic diet. Clinically, the ketogenic diet is used in neurologic medicine, most notably to reduce hard-to-control seizures in children. Studies also suggest possible benefits in other brain conditions such as Parkinson's and Alzheimer's diseases.

Fairly recently, the diet was introduced as a weight-loss diet by an Italian professor of surgery, Dr. Gianfranco Cappello of Sapienza University in Rome. In his 2012 study, about 19,000 dieters received a high-fat liquid diet via a feeding tube inserted down the nose. The study showed an average weight loss of more than 20 pounds in participants, most of whom kept it off for at least a year. The researchers reported a few minor side effects, like fatigue.

The medical community is taking note of the high public interest in keto. An article in the Jan. 16, 2018, Journal of the American Medical Association summarized several areas of promise: Many people feel less hungry on the high-fat keto diet and so may naturally reduce their overall calorie intake. Beyond weight loss, there was good news for diabetes management, with improved insulin sensitivity and blood-sugar control for people following a ketogenic diet in an early, still-ongoing study. However, an editorial appearing online July 15, 2019, in JAMA Internal Medicine concluded that "enthusiasm outpaces evidence" when it comes to a keto diet for obesity and diabetes.

Today, several versions of the keto diet (using real food) are detailed in books, blogs, and Facebook posts. The common thread is choosing high-fat foods coupled with very low daily carbs. Guidebooks include "The Complete Ketogenic Diet for Beginners" by Amy Ramos and "The Keto Diet: The Complete Guide to a High-Fat Diet" by Leanne Vogel.

How does it work?

The keto diet plan aims to force your body kind of fuel, rather than to rely upon sugar (sugar) which comes from carbs (for example, grains, legumes, vegetables (and fruits), the keto diet depends upon ketone bodies, a kind of fuel which the liver generates stored fat.

Burning fat seems to shed weight. However, the liver to generate ketone bodies is catchy:

It demands that you deprive yourself fewer than 20 to 50 g of carbohydrates every day (remember a medium-sized banana contains about 27 grams of carbohydrates).

It requires a couple of days to achieve a state of ketosis.

Ketosis can be interfered with by too much protein.

Benefits of the keto diet?

There is a ton of hype surrounding the ketogenic diet. Some researchers swear that it is the best diet for most people to be on, while others think it is just another fad diet.

To some degree, both sides of the spectrum are right. There isn't one perfect diet for everyone or every condition, regardless of how many people "believe" in it. The ketogenic diet is no exception to this rule.

However, the ketogenic diet also has plenty of solid research backing up its benefits. It is better than most diets at helping people with:

- Epilepsy

- Type 2 Diabetes
- Type 1 Diabetes
- High Blood Pressure
- Alzheimer's disease
- Parkinson's disease
- Chronic Inflammation
- High Blood Sugar Levels
- Heart Disease
- Fatty Liver Disease
- Cancer
- Migraines

Even if you are not at risk from any of these conditions, the ketogenic diet can be helpful for you too. Some of the benefits that most people experience are:

- Better brain function
- A decrease in inflammation
- An increase in energy
- Improved body composition

Healthy Fats

When advising clients on the ketogenic diet, Gioffre says he recommends seeking a ratio of 50% to 70% healthy fats. "This is where people make the biggest mistake. Healthy fats come from things like avocados, raw nuts, seeds, and extra virgin olive oil. Instead, some people see that fat is considered a good thing on the keto diet and select dairy products, eggs, cheese, butter, and bacon.

In addition to a substantial proportion of calories from fat, a keto diet should incorporate about 20% whole, organic vegetables, the diet should include 10% to 15% of calories from protein and just 5% of calories from fruit and starches. Gioffre recommends opting for plant-based proteins when possible, and if you're choosing animal proteins, select fatty fish like salmon. But be sure it's wild-caught. "Wild-caught seafood is better because farmed seafood is fed a corn and soy diet, and that creates inflammatory fats." Wild seafood has eaten a more varied diet and is thus higher in good omega-3 fatty acids.

Similarly, if you're eating land-based animal proteins, Gioffre recommends selecting grass-fed, organic, and pastured meat products. And he steers people away from chicken, which he says is "the most inflammatory of all meats."

Health Risks on Keto diet

A common complaint among people who have recently switched to a keto diet is the so-called keto flu. Symptoms include:

- Fatigue.
- Headaches.
- Muscle aches.
- Gastrointestinal distress.

It usually passes within a few days and is a sign that your body is switching to burning fat. During the week or so that people commonly experience this keto flu, it can be tough to keep up athletic performance and feel normal. Getting plenty of sleep and hydrating well can help you get over the keto flu a little faster.

Young says that the keto diet can also lead to "electrolyte imbalances, increased cholesterol, and constipation. This is why I recommend working with a dietitian to minimize these risks."

Because the keto diet is restrictive, anyone who has or has dealt with an eating disorder should skip it. Children and women who are pregnant or nursing should also avoid the keto diet. And those with kidney disease should exercise caution and get supervision before adopting this diet.

Weinandy adds that because it can impact how the body uses glucose, "people who have blood sugar issues should be cautious." Diabetics may also want to avoid the keto diet or follow it only under the close supervision of a doctor or a dietitian with special training in diabetes management. Those who are underweight or malnourished should also exercise caution, as the diet can trigger weight loss.

Shawn Wells, a registered dietitian and certified sports nutritionist based in Dallas-Fort Worth, says that for some people following the keto diet, they get too caught up in tracking macronutrient ratios and don't spend enough energy looking for high-quality food. So these individuals "tend to eat poor-quality, processed fats, which will show results in the short term but can lead to serious health issues in the long term. This is called 'dirty keto' and should be avoided." If you're relying on processed meat products and artificial sweeteners, you should take a step back and reassess your diet. "Keto diets should be focused on whole food sources to ensure that a large number of fats are coming from natural, undamaged sources,

Should you try the keto diet?

It is promoted as a miracle, but this ingestion Plan is a diet that comes with risks.

From the Sphere of diets, Focus is frequently grabbed by eating strategies. Atkins, South Beach, and the Paleo diets fit within that category. They are sometimes known as ketogenic or even "keto" diets.

However, there is a ketogenic diet different. Contrary to other A keto plan centers. Plus, it is not the kind of food to test as a test.

"Even the keto diet is primarily Utilized to help reduce the Frequency in children of seizures. Just results are analyzed while it was attempted for weight reduction, and the outcomes are mixed. We do not know whether it functions in the long run, nor if it is secure," warns registered dietitian Kathy McManus, manager of the Department of Nutrition in Harvard-affiliated Brigham and Women's Hospital.

What do you eat?

Here is a brief overview of what you should and shouldn't eat on the keto diet:

Do Not Eat

- Grains – Wheat, corn, rice, cereal, etc.
- Sugar – honey, agave, maple syrup, etc.
- Fruit – apples, bananas, oranges, etc.
- Tubers – potato, yams, etc.

Do Eat

- Meats – fish, beef, lamb, poultry, eggs, etc.
- Low-carb vegetables – spinach, kale, broccoli, etc.
- High-fat dairy – hard cheeses, high fat cream, butter, etc.
- Nuts and seeds – macadamias, walnuts, sunflower seeds, etc.
- Avocado and berries – raspberries, blackberries, and other low glycemic impact berries
- Sweeteners – stevia, erythritol, monk fruit, and other low-carb sweeteners
- Other fats – coconut oil, high-fat salad dressing, saturated fats, etc.

28-Days Keto Diet Weight Loss Challenge

First Week Meal Plan

DAYS	BREAKFAST	LUNCH	DINNER
Sunday	Simple egg porridge (Page No. 24)	Mushroom leek sauce (Page No. 67)	Creamy dijon chicken (Page No. 72)
Monday	Almond pancakes (Page No. 26)	Lunch pork pie (Page No. 52)	Tuna & cheese oven bake (Page No. 74)
Tuesday	Amazing smoothie (Page No. 29)	Shrimp scampi spinach salad (Page No. 65)	Spicy crab pot pie (Page No. 75)
Wednesday	Avocado and salmon breakfast boats (Page No. 18)	Mushroom leek sauce (Page No. 67)	Salmon & spinach casserole (Page No. 77)
Thursday	Amazing waffles (Page No. 28)	Easy stuffed avocado (Page No. 48)	Chicken provolone (Page No. 69)
Friday	Breakfast chia pudding (Page No. 22)	Lunch pork pie (Page No. 52)	Baked jalapeno poppers (Page No. 88)
Saturday	Avocado and salmon breakfast boats (Page No. 18)	Amazing chicken salad (Page No. 46)	Tomato & leek bake (Page No. 75)

28-Days Keto Diet Weight Loss Challenge

Second Week Meal Plan

DAYS	BREAKFAST	LUNCH	DINNER
Sunday	Avocado and salmon breakfast boats (Page No. 18)	Zucchini noodles soup (Page No. 55)	Bacon & egg pick-me-up (Page No. 89)
Monday	Breakfast cereal nibs (Page No. 22)	Pesto chicken salad (Page No. 49)	Chicken provolone (Page No. 69)
Tuesday	Amazing smoothie (Page No. 29)	Mushroom leek sauce (Page No. 67)	Hoisin turkey lettuce wraps (Page No. 82)
Wednesday	Breakfast chia pudding (Page No. 22)	Amazing chicken salad (Page No. 46)	Tomato & leek bake (Page No. 75)
Thursday	Amazing chicken omelet (Page No. 33)	Shrimp scampi spinach salad (Page No. 65)	Creamy dijon chicken (Page No. 72)
Friday	Avocado and salmon breakfast boats (Page No. 18)	Zucchini noodles soup (Page No. 55)	Tuna & cheese oven bake (Page No. 74)
Saturday	Simple egg porridge (Page No. 24)	Easy stuffed avocado (Page No. 48)	Baked jalapeno poppers (Page No. 88)

28-Days Keto Diet Weight Loss Challenge

Third Week Meal Plan

DAYS	BREAKFAST	LUNCH	DINNER
Sunday	Amazing chicken omelet (Page No. 33)	Amazing chicken salad (Page No. 46)	Chicken nicoise salad (Page No. 78)
Monday	Breakfast chia pudding (Page No. 22)	Mushroom leek sauce (Page No. 67)	Spicy crab pot pie (Page No. 75)
Tuesday	Avocado and salmon breakfast boats (Page No. 18)	Delicious steak bowl (Page No. 57)	Tomato & leek bake (Page No. 75)
Wednesday	Amazing smoothie (Page No. 29)	Shrimp scampi spinach salad (Page No. 65)	Chicken provolone (Page No. 69)
Thursday	Simple egg porridge (Page No. 24)	Easy stuffed avocado (Page No. 48)	Creamy dijon chicken (Page No. 72)
Friday	Breakfast cereal nibs (Page No. 22)	Delicious steak bowl (Page No. 57)	Hoisin turkey lettuce wraps (Page No. 82)
Saturday	Avocado and salmon breakfast boats (Page No. 18)	Pesto chicken salad (Page No. 49)	Tuna & cheese oven bake (Page No. 74)

28-Days Keto Diet Weight Loss Challenge

Fourth Week Meal Plan

DAYS	BREAKFAST	LUNCH	DINNER
Sunday	Avocado and salmon breakfast boats (Page No. 18)	Meatballs and pilaf (Page No. 58)	Salmon & spinach casserole (Page No. 77)
Monday	Amazing waffles (Page No. 28)	Amazing chicken salad (Page No. 46)	Chicken nicoise salad (Page No. 78)
Tuesday	Amazing smoothie (Page No. 29)	Pesto chicken salad (Page No. 49)	Green bean & garlic bacon crumble (Page No. 80)
Wednesday	Almond pancakes (Page No. 26)	Shrimp scampi spinach salad (Page No. 65)	Tuna & cheese oven bake (Page No. 74)
Thursday	Avocado and salmon breakfast boats (Page No. 18)	Meatballs and pilaf (Page No. 58)	Creamy dijon chicken (Page No. 72)
Friday	Simple egg porridge (Page No. 24)	Pesto chicken salad (Page No. 49)	Tomato & leek bake (Page No. 75)
Saturday	Breakfast chia pudding (Page No. 22)	Easy stuffed avocado (Page No. 48)	Chicken provolone (Page No. 69)

Keto cream cheese pancakes

Preparation time: 5 minutes Cooking time: 15 minutes Servings: 6

Ingredients:

- Eggs
- Oz. Cream cheese, softened
- 1 tbsp. Sugar substitute
- 2 tsp. Vanilla extract
- Tbsp. Coconut flour
- 1½ tsp. Baking powder
- Almond milk as needed

Directions:

1. Combine the eggs, cream cheese, sugar substitute, and vanilla with a blender or mixer.
2. Add the coconut flour and baking powder. Combine well. If the batter thickens after a few minutes, add a little almond milk to thin it.
3. Heat the electric griddle to 325°F. Pour the batter in 5-inch circles.
4. Wait for the surface to bubble, and then flip. Cook for 2-4 minutes longer, or until browned.
5. Serve with the toppings of your choice, or use for sandwiches.

Nutrition Per Serving: Calories: 100, Fat: 8g, Net Carbs: 3.5g, Protein: 5g

Delicious coconut flour waffles

Preparation time: 5 minutes Cooking time: 15 minutes Servings: 4

Ingredients:

- 4 tbsp. Coconut flour
- 5 eggs, separated by white and yolk
- 1 tsp. Baking powder
- 4-5 tbsp. Granulated stevia
- 3 tbsp. Whole milk
- 1 tsp. Vanilla
- 4½ oz. Butter, melted

Directions:

1. Whisk the egg whites in a bowl until they form stiff peaks.
2. In another bowl, mix the egg yolk with the coconut flour, the stevia or sweetener, and the baking powder.
3. Add the melted butter. Do so slowly, mixing until the batter is smooth.
4. Add the milk and the vanilla.
5. Combine the mixture of the first bowl with the second one, folding it in to keep the fluffiness of the batter.
6. When the waffle maker is warmed up, pour in some waffle mixture. When it is golden brown, it's finished. Repeat until all the batter is used.

Nutrition Per Serving: Calories: 277, Fat: 22g, Net Carbs: 4.3g, Protein: 8g

Healthy vegetable breakfast hash

Preparation time: 5 minutes Cooking time: 15 minutes Servings: 1

Ingredients:

- 1 medium zucchini
- ¼ cup white onion
- 2 oz. Bacon
- 1 tbsp. Coconut oil
- Fresh parsley, chopped
- 1 large egg
- Salt to taste

Directions:

1. Slice the bacon, and peel and dice the onion and zucchini.
2. Sauté the onion over medium heat and add the bacon. Stir and cook until slightly browned.
3. Add the zucchini to the pan, and cook for 10-15 minutes.
4. When done, place the hash on a plate and add the chopped parsley.
5. Top with a fried egg or, for an egg-free version, avocado.

Nutrition Per Serving: Calories: 427, Fat: 35g, Net Carbs: 7g, Protein: 17g,

Avocado and salmon breakfast boats

Preparation time: 5 minutes Cooking time: 15 minutes Servings: 1

Ingredients:

- Avocado
- Oz. Fresh goat cheese
- 2 oz. Smoked salmon
- 2 tbsp. Lemon juice
- 2 tbsp. Of organic extra virgin olive oil A dash of sea salt

Directions:

1. Cut the avocado in half, removing the stone.
2. Mix the rest of the ingredients – the salmon, goat cheese, oil, lemon juice, and salt - in a food processor until they have a creamy consistency, and place the mixture inside the avocado.
3. Enjoy!

Nutrition Per Serving: Calories: 520, Fat: 45g, Net Carbs: 5g, Protein: 20g

Sausage casserole with vegetables

Preparation time: 5 minutes Cooking time: 15 minutes Servings: 4

Ingredients:

- 2 cups zucchini, diced
- ¼ cup onion, diced
- 1 lb. Pork sausage
- 2 cups cabbage, shredded
- 3 eggs
- 2 tbsp. Mustard
- ½ cup mayonnaise
- 1½ cups cheddar cheese, shredded 1 tbsp. Dried ground sage Cayenne pepper

Directions:

1. Preheat the oven to 375°F. Grease a casserole dish and set it aside.
2. In a large skillet on a medium heat, cook the sausage and the veggies until tender.
3. Place the mixture into the casserole dish.

4. In a separate bowl, mix the eggs, mustard, mayonnaise, sage, and pepper until combined well.
5. Add the grated cheese to the egg mixture and stir for 1 minute.
6. Pour the mix over the sausage and vegetables in the casserole dish, and top with the cheese.
7. Bake the casserole for 30 minutes, or remove it when it is bubbling around the edges and the cheese on the top is melted.

Nutrition Per Serving: Calories: 480, Fat: 42g, Net Carbs: 5g, Protein: 20g

Delicious turkey breakfast

Preparation time: 10 minutes Cooking time: 20 minutes Servings: 1

Ingredients:

- 2 avocado slices
- Salt and black pepper
- 2 bacon sliced
- 2 turkey breast slices, already cooked
- 2 tablespoons coconut oil
- 2 eggs, whisked

Directions:

1. heat up a pan over medium heat, add bacon slices and brown them for a few minutes.
2. meanwhile, heat up another pan with the oil over medium heat, add eggs, salt and pepper and scramble them.
3. divide turkey breast slices on 2 plates.
4. divide scrambled eggs on each.
5. divide bacon slices and avocado slices as well and serve.
6. Enjoy!

Nutrition Per Serving: calories 135, fat 7, fiber 2, carbs 4, protein 10

Amazing burrito

Preparation time: 10 minutes Cooking time: 15 minutes Servings: 1

Ingredients:

- 1 teaspoon coconut oil
- 1 teaspoon garlic powder
- 1 teaspoon cumin, ground
- ¼ pound beef meat, ground
- 1 teaspoon sweet paprika
- 1 teaspoon onion powder
- 1 small red onion, julienned
- 1 teaspoon cilantro, chopped
- Salt and black pepper to the taste
- 3 eggs

Directions:

1. heat up a pan over medium heat, add beef and brown for a few minutes.
2. add salt, pepper, cumin, garlic and onion powder and paprika, stir, cook for 4 minutes more and take off heat.
3. in a bowl, mix eggs with salt and pepper and whisk well.
4. heat up a pan with the oil over medium heat, add egg, spread evenly and cook for 6 minutes.
5. transfer your egg burrito to a plate, divide beef mix, add onion and cilantro, roll and serve.
6. Enjoy!

Nutrition Per Serving: calories 280, fat 12, fiber 4, carbs 7, protein 14

Amazing breakfast hash

Preparation time: 10 minutes Cooking time: 15 minutes Servings: 2

Ingredients:

- 1 tablespoon coconut oil
- 2 garlic cloves, minced
- ½ cup beef stock
- Salt and black pepper to the taste
- 1 yellow onion, chopped
- 2 cups corned beef, chopped
- 1 pound radishes, cut in quarters

Directions:

- heat up a pan with the oil over medium high heat, add onion, stir and cook for 4 minutes.
- add radishes, stir and cook for 5 minutes.
- add garlic, stir and cook for 1 minute more.

- add stock, beef, salt and pepper, stir, cook for 5 minutes, take off heat and serve.
- Enjoy!

Nutrition Per Serving: calories 240, fat 7, fiber 3, carbs 12, protein 8

Brussels sprouts delight

Preparation time: 10 minutes Cooking time: 15 minutes Servings: 3

Ingredients:

- 3 eggs
- Salt and black pepper to the taste
- 1 tablespoon ghee, melted
- 2 shallots, minced
- 2 garlic cloves, minced
- 12 ounces brussels sprouts, thinly sliced
- 2 ounces bacon, chopped
- 1 and ½ tablespoons apple cider vinegar

Directions:

1. heat up a pan over medium heat, add bacon, stir, cook until it's crispy, transfer to a plate and leave aside for now.
2. heat up the pan again over medium heat, add shallots and garlic, stir and cook for 30 seconds.
3. add brussels sprouts, salt, pepper and apple cider vinegar, stir and cook for 5 minutes.
4. return bacon to pan, stir and cook for 5 minutes more.
5. add ghee, stir and make a hole in the center.
6. crack eggs into the pan, cook until they are done and serve right away.
7. Enjoy!

Nutrition Per Serving: calories 240, fat 7, fiber 4, carbs 7, protein 12

Breakfast cereal nibs

Preparation time: 10 minutes Cooking time: 35 minutes Servings: 4

Ingredients:

- 4 tablespoons hemp hearts
- ½ cup chia seeds
- 1 cup water
- 1 tablespoon vanilla extract
- 1 tablespoon psyllium powder
- 2 tablespoons coconut oil
- 1 tablespoon swerve
- 2 tablespoons cocoa nibs

Directions:

1. in a bowl, mix chia seeds with water, stir and leave aside for 5 minutes.
2. add hemp hearts, vanilla extract, psyllium powder, oil and swerve and stir well with your mixer.
3. add cocoa nibs, and stir until you obtain a dough.
4. divide dough into 2 pieces, shape into cylinder form, place on a lined baking sheet, flatten well, cover with a parchment paper, introduce in the oven at 285 degrees f and bake for 20 minutes.
5. remove the parchment paper and bake for 25 minutes more.
6. take cylinders out of the oven, leave aside to cool down and cut into small pieces.
7. serve in the morning with some almond milk.
8. Enjoy!

Nutrition Per Serving: calories 245, fat 12, fiber 12, carbs 2, protein 9

Breakfast chia pudding

Preparation time: 5=10 minutes Cooking time: 30 minutes Servings: 2

Ingredients:

- 2 tablespoons coffee
- 2 cups water
- 1/3 cup chia seeds
- 1 tablespoon swerve
- 1 tablespoon vanilla extract
- 2 tablespoons cocoa nibs
- 1/3 cup coconut cream

Directions:

1. heat up a small pot with the water over medium heat, bring to a boil, add coffee, simmer for 15 minutes, take off heat and strain into a bowl.
2. add vanilla extract, coconut cream, swerve, cocoa nibs and chia seeds, stir well, keep in the fridge for 30 minutes, divide into 2 breakfast bowls and serve.
3. Enjoy!

Nutrition Per Serving: calories 100, fat 0.4, fiber 4, carbs 3, protein 3

Delicious hemp porridge

Preparation time: 5 minutes Cooking time: 10 minutes Servings: 1

Ingredients:

- 1 tablespoon chia seeds
- 1 cup almond milk
- 2 tablespoons flax seeds
- ½ cup hemp hearts
- ½ teaspoon cinnamon, ground
- 1 tablespoon stevia
- ¾ teaspoon vanilla extract
- ¼ cup almond flour
- 1 tablespoon hemp hearts for serving

Directions:

1. in a pan, mix almond milk with ½ cup hemp hearts, chia seeds, stevia, flax seeds, cinnamon and vanilla extract, stir well and heat up over medium heat.
2. cook for 2 minutes, take off heat, add almond flour, stir well and pour into a bowl.
3. top with 1 tablespoon hemp hearts and serve.
4. Enjoy!

Nutrition Per Serving: calories 230, fat 12, fiber 7, carbs 3, protein 43

Simple breakfast cereal

Preparation time: 10 minutes Cooking time: 10 minutes Servings: 2

Ingredients:

- ½ cup coconut, shredded
- 4 teaspoons ghee
- 2 cups almond milk
- 1 tablespoon stevia

- A pinch of salt
- 1/3 cup macadamia nuts, chopped
- 1/3 cup walnuts, chopped
- 1/3 cup flax seed

Directions:

1. heat up a pot with the ghee over medium heat, add milk, coconut, salt, macadamia nuts, walnuts, flax seed and stevia and stir well.
2. cook for 3 minutes, stir again, take off heat and leave aside for 10 minutes.
3. divide into 2 bowls and serve.
4. Enjoy!

Nutrition Per Serving: calories 140, fat 3, fiber 2, carbs 1.5, protein 7

Simple egg porridge

Preparation time: 10 minutes Cooking time: 10 minutes Servings: 2

Ingredients:

2 eggs
1 tablespoon stevia
1/3 cup heavy cream
2 tablespoons ghee, melted
A pinch of cinnamon, ground

Directions:

1. in a bowl, mix eggs with stevia and heavy cream and whisk well.
2. heat up a pan with the ghee over medium high heat, add egg mix and cook until they are done.
3. transfer to 2 bowls, sprinkle cinnamon on top and serve.
4. Enjoy!

Nutrition Per Serving: calories 340, fat 12, fiber 10, carbs 3, protein 14

Delicious pancakes

Preparation time: 5 minutes Cooking time: 15 minutes Servings: 2

Ingredients:

- ½ teaspoon cinnamon, ground
- 1 teaspoon stevia
- 2 eggs
- Cooking spray
- 2 ounces cream cheese

Directions:

1. in your blender, mix eggs with cream cheese, stevia and cinnamon and blend well.
2. heat up a pan with some cooking spray over medium high heat, pour ¼ of the batter, spread well, cook for 2 minutes, flip and cook for 1 minute more.
3. transfer to a plate and repeat the action with the rest of the batter.
4. serve them right away.
5. Enjoy!

Nutrition Per Serving: calories 344, fat 23, fiber 12, carbs 3, protein 16

Almond pancakes

Preparation time: 10 minutes Cooking time: 15 minutes Servings: 6

Ingredients:

- 6 eggs
- A pinch of salt
- ½ cup coconut flour
- ¼ cup stevia
- 1/3 cup coconut, shredded
- ½ teaspoon baking powder
- 1 cup almond milk
- ¼ cup coconut oil
- 1 teaspoon almond extract
- ¼ cup almonds, toasted
- 2 ounces cocoa chocolate
- Cooking spray

Directions:

1. in a bowl, mix coconut flour with stevia, salt, baking powder and coconut and stir.
2. add coconut oil, eggs, almond milk and the almond extract and stir well again.
3. add chocolate and almonds and whisk well again.

4. heat up a pan with cooking spray over medium heat, add 2 tablespoons batter, spread into a circle, cook until it's golden, flip, cook again until it's done and transfer to a pan.
5. repeat with the rest of the batter and serve your pancakes right away.
6. Enjoy!

Nutrition Per Serving: calories 266, fat 13, fiber 8, carbs 10, protein 11

Delicious pumpkin pancakes

Preparation time: 10 minutes Cooking time: 15 minutes Servings: 6

Ingredients:

- 1-ounce egg white protein
- 2 ounces hazelnut flour
- 2 ounces flax seeds, ground
- 1 teaspoon baking powder
- 1 cup coconut cream
- 1 tablespoon chai masala
- 1 teaspoon vanilla extract
- ½ cup pumpkin puree
- 3 eggs
- 5 drops stevia
- 1 tablespoon swerve
- 1 teaspoon coconut oil

Directions:

1. in a bowl, mix flax seeds with hazelnut flour, egg white protein, baking powder and chai masala and stir.
2. in another bowl, mix coconut cream with vanilla extract, pumpkin puree, eggs, stevia and swerve and stir well.
3. combine the 2 mixtures and stir well.
4. heat up a pan with the oil over medium high heat, pour 1/6 of the batter, spread into a circle, cover, reduce heat to low, cook for 3 minutes on each side and transfer to a plate.
5. repeat with the rest of the batter and serve your pumpkin pancakes right away.
6. Enjoy!

Nutrition Per Serving: calories 400, fat 23, fiber 4, carbs 5, protein 21

Simple breakfast french toast

Preparation time: 5 minutes Cooking time: 45 minutes Servings: 12

Ingredients:

- 1 cup whey protein
- 12 egg whites
- 4 ounces cream cheese
- For the french toast:
- 1 teaspoon vanilla
- ½ cup coconut milk
- 2 eggs
- 1 teaspoon cinnamon, ground
- ½ cup ghee, melted
- ½ cup almond milk
- ½ cup swerve

Directions:

1. in a bowl, mix 12 egg whites with your mixer for a few minutes.
2. add protein and stir gently.
3. add cream cheese and stir again.
4. pour this into 2 greased bread pans, introduce in the oven at 325 degrees f and bake for 45 minutes.
5. leave breads to cool down and slice them into 18 pieces.
6. in a bowl, mix 2 eggs with vanilla, cinnamon and coconut milk and whisk well.
7. dip bread slices in this mix.
8. heat up a pan with some coconut oil over medium heat, add bread slices, cook until they are golden on each side and divide between plates.
9. heat up a pan with the ghee over high heat, add almond milk and heat up well.
10. add swerve, stir and take off heat.
11. leave aside to cool down a bit and drizzle over french toasts.
12. Enjoy!

Nutrition Per Serving: calories 200, fat 12, fiber 1, carbs 1, protein 7

Amazing waffles

Preparation time: 10 minutes Cooking time: 20 minutes Servings: 4

Ingredients:

- 4 eggs, separated
- 3 tablespoons almond milk
- 1 teaspoon baking powder
- 3 tablespoons stevia

- 4 tablespoons coconut flour
- 2 teaspoon vanilla
- 4 ounces ghee, melted

Directions:

1. in a bowl, whisk egg white using your mixer.
2. in another bowl mix flour with stevia, baking powder and egg yolks and whisk well.
3. add vanilla, ghee and milk and stir well again.
4. add egg white and stir gently everything.
5. pour some of the mix into your waffle maker and cook until it's golden.
6. repeat with the rest of the batter and serve your waffles right away.
7. Enjoy!

Nutrition Per Serving: calories 240, fat 23, fiber 2, carbs 4, protein 7

Baked granola

Preparation time: 10 minutes Cooking time: 55 minutes Servings: 4

Ingredients:

- ½ cup almonds, chopped
- 1 cup pecans, chopped
- ½ cup walnuts, chopped
- ½ cup coconut, flaked
- ¼ cup flax meal
- ½ cup almond milk
- ¼ cup sunflower seeds
- ¼ cup pepitas
- ½ cup stevia
- ¼ cup ghee, melted
- 1 teaspoon honey
- 1 teaspoon vanilla
- 1 teaspoon cinnamon, ground
- A pinch of salt
- ½ teaspoon nutmeg
- ¼ cup water

Directions:

1. in a bowl, mix almonds with pecans, walnuts, coconut, flax meal, milk, sunflower seeds, pepitas, stevia, ghee, honey, vanilla, cinnamon, salt, nutmeg and water and whisk very well.
2. grease a baking sheet with parchment paper, spread granola mix and press well.
3. cover with another piece of parchment paper, introduce in the oven at 250 degrees f and bake for 1 hour.
4. take granola out of the oven, leave aside to cool down, break into pieces and serve.
5. Enjoy!

Nutrition Per Serving: calories 340, fat 32, fiber 12, carbs 20, protein 20

Amazing smoothie

Preparation time: 5 minutes Cooking time: 10 minutes Servings: 2

Ingredients:

- 2 brazil nuts
- 1 cup coconut milk
- 10 almonds
- 2 cups spinach leaves
- 1 teaspoon green powder
- 1 teaspoon whey protein
- 1 tablespoon psyllium seeds
- 1 tablespoon potato starch

Directions:

1. in your blender, mix spinach with brazil nuts, coconut milk and almonds and blend well.
2. add green powder, whey protein, potato starch and psyllium seeds and blend well again.
3. pour into a tall glass and consume for breakfast.
4. Enjoy!

Nutrition Per Serving: calories 340, fat 30, fiber 7, carbs 7, protein 12

Refreshing breakfast smoothie

Preparation time: 5 minutes Cooking time: 10 minutes Servings: 4

Ingredients:

- 1 cup lettuce leaves
- 4 cups water
- 2 tablespoons parsley leaves
- 1 tablespoon ginger, grated
- 1 tablespoon swerve
- 1 cup cucumber, sliced
- ½ avocado, pitted and peeled
- ½ cup kiwi, peeled and sliced
- 1/3 cup pineapple, chopped

Directions:

1. in your blender, mix water with lettuce leaves, pineapple, parsley, cucumber, ginger, kiwi, avocado and swerve and blend very well.

2. pour into glasses and serve for a keto breakfast.
3. Enjoy!

Nutrition Per Serving: calories 60, fat 2, fiber 3, carbs 3, protein 1

Amazing breakfast in a glass

Preparation time: 5 minutes Cooking time: 10 minutes Servings: 2

Ingredients:

- 10 ounces canned coconut milk
- 1 cup favorite greens
- ¼ cup cocoa nibs
- 1 cup water
- 1 cup cherries, frozen
- ¼ cup cocoa powder
- 1 small avocado, pitted and peeled
- ¼ teaspoon turmeric

Directions:

1. in your blender, mix coconut milk with avocado, cocoa powder, cherries and turmeric and blend well.
2. add water, greens and cocoa nibs, blend for 2 minutes more, pour into glasses and serve.
3. Enjoy!

Nutrition Per Serving: calories 100, fat 3, fiber 2, carbs 3, protein 5

Delicious chicken quiche

Preparation time: 10 minutes Cooking time: 45 minutes Servings: 6

Ingredients:

- 6 eggs
- 2 cups almond flour
- 2 tablespoons coconut oil
- Salt and black pepper to the taste
- 2 zucchinis, grated
- ½ cup heavy cream
- 1 teaspoon fennel seeds
- 1 teaspoon oregano, dried
- 1 pound chicken meat, ground

Directions:

1. in your food processor, blend almond flour with a pinch of salt.
2. add 1 egg and coconut oil and blend well.
3. place dough in a greased pie pan and press well on the bottom.
4. heat up a pan over medium heat, add chicken meat, brown for a couple of minutes, take off heat and leave aside.
5. in a bowl, mix 6 eggs with salt, pepper, oregano, cream and fennel seeds and whisk well.
6. add chicken meat and stir again.
7. pour this into pie crust, spread, introduce in the oven at 350 degrees f and bake for 40 minutes.
8. leave the pie to cool down a bit before slicing and serving it for breakfast!
9. Enjoy!

Nutrition Per Serving: calories 300, fat 23, fiber 3, carbs 4, protein 18

Delicious steak and eggs

Preparation time: 10 minutes Cooking time: 10 minutes Servings: 1

Ingredients:

- 4 ounces sirloin
- 1 small avocado, pitted, peeled and sliced
- 3 eggs
- 1 tablespoon ghee
- Salt and black pepper to the taste

Directions:

1. heat up a pan with the ghee over medium high heat, crack eggs into the pan and cook them as you wish.
2. season with salt and pepper, take off heat and transfer to a plate.
3. heat up another pan over medium high heat, add sirloin, cook for 4 minutes, take off heat, leave aside to cool down and cut into thin strips.

4. season with salt and pepper to the taste and place next to the eggs.
5. add avocado slices on the side and serve.
6. Enjoy!

Nutrition Per Serving: calories 500, fat 34, fiber 10, carbs 3, protein 40

Amazing chicken omelet

Preparation time: 10 minutes Cooking time: 10 minutes Servings: 1

Ingredients:

- 1 ounce rotisserie chicken, shredded
- 1 teaspoon mustard
- 1 tablespoon homemade mayonnaise
- 1 tomato, chopped
- 2 bacon slices, cooked and crumbled
- 2 eggs
- 1 small avocado, pitted, peeled and chopped
- Salt and black pepper to the taste

Directions:

1. in a bowl, mix eggs with some salt and pepper and whisk gently.
2. heat up a pan over medium heat, spray with some cooking oil, add eggs and cook your omelet for 5 minutes.
3. add chicken, avocado, tomato, bacon, mayo and mustard on one half of the omelet.
4. fold omelet, cover pan and cook for 5 minutes more.
5. transfer to a plate and serve.
6. Enjoy!

Nutrition Per Serving: calories 400, fat 32, fiber 6, carbs 4, protein 25

Simple smoothie bowl

Preparation time: 10 minutes Cooking time: 5 minutes Servings: 1

Ingredients:

- 2 ice cubes
- 1 tablespoon coconut oil
- 2 tablespoons heavy cream
- 1 cup spinach
- ½ cup almond milk
- 1 teaspoon protein powder
- 4 raspberries
- 1 tablespoon coconut ,shredded

- 4 walnuts
- 1 teaspoon chia seeds

1. in your blender, mix milk with spinach, cream, ice, protein powder and coconut oil, blend well and transfer to a bowl.
2. top your bowl with raspberries, coconut, walnuts and chia seeds and serve.
3. Enjoy!

Nutrition Per Serving: calories 450, fat 34, fiber 4, carbs 4, protein 35

Keto lemon muffins with poppy seeds

Preparation time: 5 minutes Cooking time: 15 minutes Servings: 12

Ingredients:

- ¾ cup almond flour
- ⅓ cup Erythritol ¼ cup Flaxseed meal
- 1 tbsp. Baking powder
- 2 tbsp. Poppy seeds
- Cup Butter, melted 3 eggs
- Cup Heavy cream 3 tbsp. Lemon juice
- Lemon zest of 2 lemons 1 tbsp. Vanilla
- 20 drops liquid sweetener

Directions:

1. Preheat the oven to 345°F.
2. Meanwhile, mix in a bowl the flaxseed meal, almond flour, erythritol and poppy seeds.
3. Add melted butter, and mix in the eggs and heavy cream until it reaches a smooth consistency. Add the rest of the ingredients and mix.
4. Place the batter into the muffin pan (divided into 12) and bake them for 18-20 minutes.
5. Remove from the oven and cool for approximately 10 minutes.

Nutrition Per Serving: Calories: 130, Fat: 11.5g, Net Carbs: 1.7g, Protein: 4g

Breakfast tacos

Preparation time: 5 minutes Cooking time: 15 minutes Servings: 2

Ingredients:

- 1 cup mozzarella cheese, shredded
- 6 eggs
- 2 tbsp. Butter
- 3 strips of bacon
- 1 oz. Cheddar cheese, shredded
- ½ an avocado
- Salt and pepper

Directions:

1. Cook the bacon on a baking sheet covered with aluminum foil at 375°F, until crispy (12-15 minutes).
2. Meanwhile, use a third of the mozzarella to cover the bottom of a nonstick pan. Heat for 2-3 minutes on medium heat, or until the edges begin to brown.
3. With a pair of tongs, remove the mozzarella from the pan (it will now be a taco shell). Repeat with the remaining cheese.
4. Scramble the eggs in the butter. Stir frequently, and add pepper and salt to taste.
5. Fill the shells with the eggs, avocado and bacon. Sprinkle cheddar cheese on the top. Add hot sauce or cilantro (optional).

Nutrition Per Serving: Calories: 440, Fat: 36g, Net Carbs: 4g, Protein: 26g,

Cheddar and bacon omelets

Preparation time: 5 minutes Cooking time: 15 minutes Servings: 1

Ingredients:

- 2 slices of bacon
- 2 tbsp. Bacon grease
- 2 eggs
- 2 stalks of chives
- 1 oz. Cheddar cheese Salt and pepper

Directions:

1. Place the bacon fat in a pre-heated pan on a medium-low heat, and let it melt. Add the eggs, chives, salt and pepper. Stir lightly.
2. Add the bacon once the edges are set. Cook for 20-30 seconds more.
3. Add cheese to the omelet and fold in half. Flip over and warm through on the other side.

Nutrition Per Serving: Calories: 460, Fat: 40g, Net Carbs: 2g, Protein: 25g

Pumpkin bread

Preparation time: 10 minutes Cooking time: 20 minutes Servings: 10

Ingredients:

- 1½ cups almond flour
- 3 egg whites
- Cup granulated sugar
- ½ cup coconut milk
- Cup psyllium husk powder
- 1½ tsp. Pumpkin pie spice
- 2 tsp. Baking powder
- ½ tsp. Salt

Directions:

1. In a bowl, sift all the dry ingredients. Place a container with 1 cup of water into a preheated oven (350°F).
2. Add the pumpkin and coconut milk to the dry ingredients, and mix.
3. Whisk the egg whites, and add them into the dough, folding carefully.
4. Place the dough into a greased loaf pan, and cook the bread for 75 minutes.

Nutrition Per Serving: Calories: 120, Fat: 9g, Net Carbs: 3g, Protein: 5g

Salted caramel cereal with pork rinds

Preparation time: 5 minutes Cooking time: 15 minutes Servings: 2

Ingredients:

- 1 oz. Pork rinds
- 2 tbsp. Butter
- 1 cup vanilla coconut milk
- 2 tbsp. Heavy cream
- ¼ tbsp. Ground cinnamon
- 1 tbsp. Erythritol

Directions:

1. In a pan on a medium heat, add the butter and stir until browned.
2. Remove and add the heavy cream and erythritol. Mix well and return to the heat. Continue heating, stirring constantly until the desired caramel color is achieved.
3. Add the pork rinds and mix them in, being careful to coat evenly.
4. Place them into a container and put in the fridge for 20-45 minutes to cool them down.

Nutrition Per Serving: Calories: 510, Fat: 50g, Net Carbs: 2.7g, Protein: 15g

Delicious lunch pizza

Preparation time: 10 minutes cooking time: 7 minutes servings: 4

Ingredients:

- 1 cup pizza cheese mix, shredded
- 1 tablespoon olive oil
- 2 tablespoons ghee
- 1 cup mozzarella cheese, shredded
- ¼ cup mascarpone cheese
- 1 tablespoon heavy cream
- 1 teaspoon garlic, minced
- Salt and black pepper to the taste
- A pinch of lemon pepper
- 1/3 cup broccoli florets, steamed
- Some asiago cheese, shaved for serving

Directions:

1. heat up a pan with the oil over medium heat, add pizza cheese mix and spread into a circle.
2. add mozzarella cheese and also spread into a circle.
3. cook everything for 5 minutes and transfer to a plate.
4. heat up the pan with the ghee over medium heat, add mascarpone cheese, cream, salt, pepper, lemon pepper and garlic, stir and cook for 5 minutes.
5. drizzle half of this mix over cheese crust.
6. add broccoli florets to the pan with the rest of the mascarpone mix, stir and cook for 1 minute.
7. add this on top of the pizza, sprinkle asiago cheese at the end and serve.
8. Enjoy!

Nutrition Per Serving: calories 250, fat 15, fiber 1, carbs 3, protein 10

Simple pizza rolls

Preparation time: 10 minutes cooking time: 30 minutes servings: 6

Ingredients:

- ¼ cup mixed red and green bell peppers, chopped
- 2 cup mozzarella cheese, shredded
- 1 teaspoon pizza seasoning
- 2 tablespoons onion, chopped
- 1 tomato, chopped
- Salt and black pepper to the taste
- ¼ cup pizza sauce
- ½ cup sausage, crumbled and cooked

Directions:

1. spread mozzarella cheese on a lined and lightly greased baking sheet, sprinkle pizza seasoning on top, introduce in the oven at 400 degrees f and bake for 20 minutes.
2. take your pizza crust out of the oven, spread sausage, onion, bell peppers and tomatoes all over and drizzle the tomato sauce at the end.
3. introduce in the oven again and bake for 10 minutes more.
4. take pizza out of the oven, leave aside for a couple of minutes, slice into 6 pieces, roll each piece and serve for lunch!
5. Enjoy!

Nutrition Per Serving: calories 117, fat 7, fiber 1, carbs 2, protein 11

Delicious lunch dish

Preparation time: 10 minutes cooking time: 15 minutes servings: 2

Ingredients:

- 1 and ½ cups cheddar cheese, shredded
- 1 and ½ cups cheese blend
- 2 beef hot dogs, finely chopped
- A drizzle of olive oil
- 1 pound beef meat, ground
- Salt and black pepper to the taste
- ¼ teaspoon paprika
- ¼ teaspoon old bay
- ¼ teaspoon onion powder
- ¼ teaspoon garlic powder

- 1 cup lettuce leaves, chopped
- 1 tablespoon thousand island dressing
- 2 tablespoons dill pickle, chopped
- 2 tablespoons yellow onion, chopped
- ½ cup american cheese, shredded
- Some ketchup for serving
- Some mustard for serving

Directions:

1. heat up a pan with a drizzle of oil over medium heat, add half of the cheese blend, spread into a circle and top with half of the cheddar cheese.
2. also spread into a circle, cook for 5 minutes, transfer to a cutting board and leave aside for a few minutes to cool down.
3. heat up the pan again, add the rest of the cheese blend and spread into a circle.
4. add the rest of the cheddar, also spread, cook for 5 minutes and also transfer to a cutting board.
5. spread the thousand island dressing over the 2 pizza crusts.
6. heat up the same pan again over medium heat, add beef, stir and brown for a few minutes.
7. add salt, pepper, old bay seasoning, paprika, onion and garlic powder, stir and cook for a few minutes more.
8. add hot dogs pieces, stir and cook for 5 minutes more.
9. pread lettuce, pickles, american cheese and onions on the 2 pizza crusts.
10. divide beef and hot dog mix, drizzle mustard and ketchup at the end and serve.

Nutrition Per Serving: calories 200, fat 6, fiber 3, carbs 1.5, protein 10

Delicious mexican lunch

Preparation time: 10 minutes cooking time: 20 minutes servings: 4

Ingredients:

- ¼ cup cilantro, chopped
- 2 avocados, pitted, peeled and cut into chunks
- 1 tablespoon lime juice
- ¼ cup white onion, chopped
- 1 teaspoon garlic, minced
- Salt and black pepper to the taste
- 6 cherry tomatoes, cut in quarters
- ½ cup water
- 2-pound beef meat, ground
- 2 cups sour cream
- ¼ cup taco seasoning
- 2 cups lettuce leaves, shredded
- Some cayenne pepper sauce for serving
- 2 cups cheddar cheese, shredded

Directions:

1. in a bowl, mix cilantro with lime juice, avocado, onion, tomatoes, salt, pepper and garlic, stir well and leave aside in the fridge for now.
2. heat up a pan over medium heat, add beef, stir and brown for 10 minutes.
3. add taco seasoning and water, stir and cook over medium-low heat for 10 minutes more.
4. divide this mix into 4 serving bowls.
5. add sour cream, avocado mix you've made earlier, lettuce pieces and cheddar cheese.
6. drizzle cayenne pepper sauce at the end and serve for lunch!
7. Enjoy!

Nutrition Per Serving: calories 340, fat 30, fiber 5, carbs 3, protein 32

Lunch stuffed peppers

Preparation time: 10 minutes cooking time: 40 minutes servings: 4

Ingredients:

- 4 big banana peppers
- 1 tablespoon ghee
- Salt and black pepper to the taste
- ½ teaspoon herbs de provence
- 1 pound sweet sausage, chopped
- 3 tablespoons yellow onions, chopped
- Some marinara sauce a drizzle of olive oil

Directions:

1. season banana peppers with salt and pepper, drizzle the oil, rub well and bake in the oven at 350 degrees f for 20 minutes.
2. meanwhile, heat up a pan over medium heat, add sausage pieces, stir and cook for 5 minutes.
3. add onion, herbs de provence, salt, pepper and ghee, stir well and cook for 5 minutes.
4. take peppers out of the oven, fill them with the sausage mix, place them in an oven-proof dish, drizzle marinara sauce over them, introduce in the oven again and bake for 10 minutes more.serve hot.
5. Enjoy!

Nutrition Per Serving: calories 320, fat 8, fiber 4, carbs 3, protein 10

Special lunch burgers

Preparation time: 10 minutes cooking time: 25 minutes servings: 8

Ingredients:

- 1 pound brisket, ground
- 1 pound beef, ground
- Salt and black pepper to the taste
- 8 butter slices
- 1 tablespoon garlic, minced
- 1 tablespoon italian seasoning
- 2 tablespoons mayonnaise
- 1 tablespoon ghee
- 2 tablespoons olive oil
- 1 yellow onion, chopped
- 1 tablespoon water

Directions:

1. in a bowl, mix brisket with beef, salt, pepper, italian seasoning, garlic and mayo and stir well.
2. shape 8 patties and make a pocket in each.
3. stuff each burger with a butter slice and seal.
4. heat up a pan with the olive oil over medium heat, add onions, stir and cook for 2 minutes.
5. add the water, stir and gather them in the corner of the pan.
6. place burgers in the pan with the onions and cook them over medium-low heat for 10 minutes.
7. flip them, add the ghee and cook them for 10 minutes more.
8. divide burgers on buns and serve them with caramelized onions on top.
9. Enjoy!

Nutrition Per Serving: calories 180, fat 8, fiber 1, carbs 4, protein 20

Different burger

Preparation time: 10 minutes cooking time: 30 minutes servings: 4

Ingredients:

- 4 chili peppers, chopped
- 1 cup water
- 1 cup almond butter
- 1 teaspoon swerve
- 6 tablespoons coconut aminos
- 4 garlic cloves, minced
- 1 tablespoon rice vinegar
- For the burgers:
- 4 pepper jack cheese slices
- 1 and ½ pounds beef, ground
- 1 red onion, sliced
- 8 bacon slices
- 8 lettuce leaves
- Salt and black pepper to the taste

Directions:

1. Heat up a pan with the almond butter over medium heat.

2. add water, stir well and bring to a simmer.
3. add coconut aminos and stir well.
4. in your food processor, mix chili peppers with garlic, swerve and vinegar and blend well.
5. add this to almond butter mix, stir well, take off heat and leave aside for now.
6. in a bowl, mix beef with salt and pepper, stir and shape 4 patties.
7. place them in a pan, introduce in your preheated broiler and broil for 7 minutes.
8. flip burgers and broil them for 7 minutes more.
9. place cheese slices on burgers, introduce in your broiler and broil for 4 minutes more.
10. heat up a pan over medium heat, add bacon slices and fry them for a couple of minutes.
11. place 2 lettuce leaves on a dish, add 1 burger on top, then 1
12. Onion slice and 1 bacon slice and top with some almond butter sauce.
13. repeat with the rest of the lettuce leaves, burgers, onion, bacon and sauce.
14. Enjoy!

Nutrition Per Serving: calories 700, fat 56, fiber 10, carbs 7, protein 40

Delicious zucchini dish

Preparation time: 10 minutes cooking time: 5 minutes servings: 1

Ingredients:

- 1 tablespoon olive oil
- 3 tablespoons ghee
- 2 cups zucchini, cut with a spiralizer
- 1 teaspoon red pepper flakes
- 1 tablespoon garlic, minced
- 1 tablespoon red bell pepper, chopped
- Salt and black pepper to the taste
- 1 tablespoon basil, chopped
- ¼ cup asiago cheese, shaved
- ¼ cup parmesan, grated

Directions:

1. heat up a pan with the oil and ghee over medium heat, add garlic, bell pepper and pepper flakes, stir and cook for 1 minute.
2. add zucchini noodles, stir and cook for 2 minutes more.

3. add basil, parmesan, salt and pepper, stir and cook for a few seconds more.
4. take off heat, transfer to a bowl and serve for lunch with asiago cheese on top.
5. Enjoy!

Nutrition Per Serving: calories 140, fat 3, fiber 1, carbs 1.3, protein 5

Bacon and zucchini noodles salad

Preparation time: 10 minutes cooking time: 0 minutes servings: 2

Ingredients:

- 1 cup baby spinach
- 4 cups zucchini noodles
- 1/3 cup bleu cheese, crumbled
- 1/3 cup thick cheese dressing
- ½ cup bacon, cooked and crumbled
- Black pepper to the taste

Directions:

1. in a salad bowl, mix spinach with zucchini noodles, bacon and bleu cheese and toss.
2. add cheese dressing and black pepper to the taste, toss well to coat, divide into 2 bowls and serve.
3. Enjoy!

Nutrition Per Serving: calories 200, fat 14, fiber 4, carbs 2, protein 10

Amazing chicken salad

Preparation time: 10 minutes cooking time: 0 minutes servings: 3

Ingredients:

- 1 green onion, chopped
- 1 celery rib, chopped
- 1 egg, hard-boiled, peeled and chopped
- 5 ounces chicken breast, roasted and chopped
- 2 tablespoons parsley, chopped
- ½ tablespoons dill relish

- Salt and black pepper to the taste
- 1/3 cup mayonnaise
- A pinch of granulated garlic
- 1 teaspoon mustard

Directions:

1. In your food processor, mix parsley with onion and celery and pulse well.
2. transfer these to a bowl and leave aside for now.
3. put chicken meat in your food processor, blend well and add to the bowl with the veggies.
4. add egg pieces, salt and pepper and stir.
5. also add mustard, mayo, dill relish and granulated garlic, toss to coat and serve right away.
6. Enjoy!

Nutrition Per Serving: calories 283, fat 23, fiber 5, carbs 3, protein 12

Unbelievable steak salad

Preparation time: 10 minutes cooking time: 20 minutes servings: 4

Ingredients:

- 1 and ½ pound steak, thinly sliced
- 3 tablespoons avocado oil
- Salt and black pepper to the taste
- ¼ cup balsamic vinegar
- 6 ounces sweet onion, chopped
- 1 lettuce head, chopped
- 2 garlic cloves, minced
- 4 ounces mushrooms, sliced
- 1 avocado, pitted, peeled and sliced
- 3 ounces sun-dried tomatoes, chopped
- 1 yellow bell pepper, sliced
- 1 orange bell pepper, sliced
- 1 teaspoon italian seasoning
- 1 teaspoon red pepper flakes
- 1 teaspoon onion powder

Directions:

1. In a bowl, mix steak pieces with some salt, pepper and balsamic vinegar, toss to coat and leave aside for now.
2. heat up a pan with the avocado oil over medium-low heat, add mushrooms, garlic, salt, pepper and onion, stir and cook for 20 minutes.
3. in a bowl, mix lettuce leaves with orange and yellow bell pepper, sun dried tomatoes and avocado and stirred.
4. season steak pieces with onion powder, pepper flakes and italian seasoning.
5. place steak pieces in a broiling pan, introduce in preheated broiler and cook for 5 minutes.
6. divide steak pieces on plates, add lettuce and avocado salad on the side and top everything with onion and mushroom mix.
7. Enjoy!

Nutrition Per Serving: calories 435, fat 23, fiber 7, carbs 10, protein 35

Fennel and chicken lunch salad

Preparation time: 10 minutes cooking time: 0 minutes servings: 4

Ingredients:

3 chicken breasts, boneless, skinless, cooked and chopped
2 tablespoons walnut oil
¼ cup walnuts, toasted and chopped
1 and ½ cup fennel, chopped
2 tablespoons lemon juice
¼ cup mayonnaise
2 tablespoons fennel fronds, chopped
Salt and black pepper to the taste a pinch of cayenne pepper

Directions:

1. In a bowl, mix fennel with chicken and walnuts and stir.
2. in another bowl, mix mayo with salt, pepper, fennel fronds, walnut oil, lemon juice, cayenne and garlic and stir well.
3. pour this over chicken and fennel mix, toss to coat well and keep in the fridge until you serve.
4. Enjoy!

Nutrition Per Serving: calories 200, fat 10, fiber 1, carbs 3, protein 7

Easy stuffed avocado

Preparation time: 10 minutes cooking time: 0 minutes servings: 1

Ingredients:

- 1 avocado
- 4 ounces canned sardines, drained
- 1 spring onion, chopped
- 1 tablespoon mayonnaise
- 1 tablespoon lemon juice
- Salt and black pepper to the taste
- ¼ teaspoon turmeric powder

Directions:

1. Cut avocado in halves, scoop flesh and put in a bowl.
2. mash with a fork and mix with sardines.
3. mash again with your fork and mix with onion, lemon juice, turmeric powder, salt, pepper and mayo.
4. stir everything and divide into avocado halves.
5. serve for lunch right away.
6. Enjoy!

Nutrition Per Serving: calories 230, fat 34, fiber 12, carbs 5, protein 27

Pesto chicken salad

Preparation time: 10 minutes cooking time: 0 minutes servings: 4

Ingredients:

- 1 pound chicken meat, cooked and cubed
- Salt and black pepper to the taste
- 10 cherry tomatoes, halved
- 6 bacon slices, cooked and crumbled
- ¼ cup mayonnaise
- 1 avocado, pitted, peeled and cubed
- 2 tablespoons garlic pesto

Directions:

1. In a salad bowl, mix chicken with bacon, avocado, tomatoes, salt and pepper and stir.
2. Add mayo and garlic pesto, toss well to coat and serve.
3. Enjoy!

Nutrition Per Serving: calories 357, fat 23, fiber 5, carbs 3, protein 26

Tasty lunch salad

Preparation time: 10 minutes cooking time: 10 minutes servings: 1

Ingredients:

- 4 ounces beef steak
- 2 cups lettuce leaves, shredded
- Salt and black pepper to the taste
- Cooking spray
- 2 tablespoons cilantro, chopped
- 2 radishes, sliced
- 1/3 cup red cabbage, shredded
- 3 tablespoons jarred chimichurri sauce
- 1 tablespoons salad dressing
- For the salad dressing:
- 3 garlic cloves, minced
- ½ teaspoon worcestershire sauce
- 1 tablespoon mustard
- ½ cup apple cider vinegar
- ¼ cup water
- ½ cup olive oil
- ¼ teaspoon tabasco sauce
- Salt and black pepper to the taste

Directions:

1. In a bowl, mix garlic cloves with worcestershire sauce, mustard, cider vinegar, water, olive oil, salt, pepper and tabasco sauce, whisk well and leave aside for now.
2. heat up your kitchen grill over medium high heat, spray cooking oil, add steak, season with salt and pepper, cook for 4 minutes, flip, cook for 4 minutes more, take off heat, leave aside to cool down and cut into thin strips.
3. in a salad bowl, mix lettuce with cilantro, cabbage, radishes, chimichurri sauce and steak strips.
4. add 1 tablespoons of salad dressing, toss to coat and serve right away.

Nutrition Per Serving: calories 456, fat 32, fiber 2, carbs 6, protein 30

Easy lunch crab cakes

Preparation time: 10 minutes cooking time: 12 minutes servings: 6

Ingredients:

- 1 pound crabmeat
- ¼ cup parsley, chopped
- Salt and black pepper to the taste
- 2 green onions, chopped
- ¼ cup cilantro, chopped
- 1 teaspoon jalapeno pepper, minced
- 1 teaspoon lemon juice
- 1 teaspoon worcestershire sauce
- 1 teaspoon old bay seasoning
- ½ teaspoon mustard powder
- ½ cup mayonnaise
- 1 egg
- 2 tablespoons olive oil

Directions:

1. In a large bowl mix crab meat with salt, pepper, parsley, green onions, cilantro, jalapeno, lemon juice, old bay seasoning, mustard powder and worcestershire sauce and stir very well.
2. in another bowl mix egg wit mayo and whisk.
3. add this to crabmeat mix and stir everything.
4. shape 6 patties from this mix and place them on a plate.
5. heat up a pan with the oil over medium high heat, add 3 crab cakes, cook for 3 minutes, flip, cook them for 3 minutes more and transfer to paper towels.
6. repeat with the other 3 crab cakes, drain excess grease and serve for lunch.
7. Enjoy!

Nutrition Per Serving: calories 254, fat 17, fiber 1, carbs 1, protein 20

Easy lunch muffins

Preparation time: 10 minutes cooking time: 45 minutes servings: 13

Ingredients:

- 6 egg yolks
- 2 tablespoons coconut aminos
- ½ pound mushrooms
- ¾ cup coconut flour
- 1 pound beef, ground
- Salt to the taste

Directions:

1. In your food processor, mix mushrooms with salt, coconut aminos and egg yolks and blend well.
2. in a bowl, mix beef meat with some salt and stir.
3. add mushroom mix to beef and stir everything.
4. add coconut flour and stir again.
5. divide this into 13 cupcake cups, introduce in the oven at 350 degrees f and bake for 45 minutes.
6. Enjoy!

Nutrition Per Serving: calories 160, fat 10, fiber 3, carbs 1, protein 12

Lunch pork pie

Preparation time: 10 minutes cooking time: 50 minutes servings: 6

Ingredients:

- 2 cups cracklings
- ¼ cup flax meal
- 1 cup almond flour
- 2 eggs
- A pinch of salt
- For the filling:
- 1 cup cheddar cheese, grated
- 4 eggs
- 12 ounces pork loin, chopped
- 6 bacon slices
- ½ cup cream cheese
- 1 red onion, chopped
- ¼ cup chives, chopped
- 2 garlic cloves, minced
- Salt and black pepper to the taste
- 2 tablespoons ghee

Directions:

1. In your food processor, mix cracklings with almond flour, flax meal, 2 eggs and salt and blend until you obtain a dough.
2. transfer this to a pie pan and press well on the bottom.
3. introduce in the oven at 350 degrees f and bake for 15 minutes.
4. meanwhile, heat up a pan with the ghee over medium high heat, add garlic and onion, stir and cook for 5 minutes.
5. add bacon, stir and cook for 5 minutes.
6. add pork loin, cook until it's brown on all sides and take off heat.
7. in a bowl, mix eggs with salt, pepper, cheddar cheese and cream cheese and blend well.
8. add chives and stir again.
9. spread pork into pie pan, add eggs mix, introduce in the oven at
10. 350 degrees f and bake for 25 minutes.
11. leave the pie to cool down for a couple of minutes and serve.

Nutrition Per Serving: calories 455, fat 34, fiber 3, carbs 3, protein 33

Delicious lunch pate

Preparation time: 10 minutes cooking time: 0 minutes servings: 1

Ingredients:

- 4 ounces chicken livers, sautéed
- 1 teaspoon mixed thyme, sage and oregano, chopped
- Salt and black pepper to the taste
- 3 tablespoons butter
- 3 radishes, thinly sliced crusted bread slices for serving

Directions:

1. In your food processor, mix chicken livers with thyme, sage, oregano, butter, salt and pepper and blend very well for a few minutes.
2. spread on crusted bread slices and top with radishes slices.
3. serve right away.
4. Enjoy!

Nutrition Per Serving: calories 380, fat 40, fiber 5, carbs 1, protein 17

Delicious lunch chowder

Preparation time: 10 minutes cooking time: 4 hours servings: 4

Ingredients:

- 1 pound chicken thighs, skinless and boneless
- 10 ounces canned tomatoes, chopped
- 1 cup chicken stock
- 8 ounces cream cheese
- Juice from 1 lime
- Salt and black pepper to the taste
- 1 jalapeno pepper, chopped
- 1 yellow onion, chopped
- 2 tablespoons cilantro, chopped
- 1 garlic clove, minced
- Cheddar cheese, shredded for serving
- Lime wedges for serving

Directions:

1. In your crock pot, mix chicken with tomatoes, stock, cream cheese, salt, pepper, lime juice, jalapeno, onion, garlic and cilantro, stir, cover and cook on high for 4 hours.
2. Uncover pot, shred meat into the pot, divide into bowls and serve with cheddar cheese on top and lime wedges on the side.
3. Enjoy!

Nutrition Per Serving: calories 300, fat 5, fiber 6, carbs 3, protein 26

Delicious coconut soup

Preparation time: 10 minutes cooking time: 30 minutes servings: 2

Ingredients:

- 4 cups chicken stock
- 3 lime leaves
- 1 and ½ cups coconut milk
- 1 teaspoon lemongrass, dried
- 1 cup cilantro, chopped
- 1 inch ginger, grated
- 4 thai chilies, dried and chopped
- Salt and black pepper to the taste
- 4 ounces shrimp, raw, peeled and deveined
- 2 tablespoons red onion, chopped
- 1 tablespoon coconut oil
- 2 tablespoons mushrooms, chopped
- 1 tablespoon fish sauce
- 1 tablespoon cilantro, chopped
- Juice from 1 lime

Directions:

1. In a pot, mix chicken stock with coconut milk, lime leaves, lemongrass, thai chilies, 1 cup cilantro, ginger, salt and pepper, stir, bring to a simmer over medium heat, cook for 20 minutes, strain and return to pot.
2. heat up soup again over medium heat, add coconut oil, shrimp, fish sauce, mushrooms and onions, stir and cook for 10 minutes more.
3. add lime juice and 1 tablespoon cilantro, stir, ladle into bowls and serve for lunch!
4. Enjoy!

Nutrition Per Serving: calories 450, fat 34, fiber 4, carbs 8, protein 12

Zucchini noodles soup

Preparation time: 10 minutes cooking time: 15 minutes servings: 8

Ingredients:

- 1 small yellow onion, chopped
- 2 garlic cloves, minced
- 1 jalapeno pepper, chopped
- 1 tablespoon coconut oil
- 1 and ½ tablespoons curry paste
- 6 cups chicken stock
- 15 ounces canned coconut milk
- 1 pound chicken breasts, sliced
- 1 red bell pepper, sliced
- 2 tablespoons fish sauce
- 2 zucchinis, cut with a spiralizer
- ½ cup cilantro, chopped
- Lime wedges for serving

Directions:

1. Heat up a pot with the oil over medium heat, add onion, stir and cook for 5 minutes.
2. add garlic, jalapeno and curry paste, stir and cook for 1 minute.
3. add stock and coconut milk, stir and bring to a boil.
4. add red bell pepper, chicken and fish sauce, stir and simmer for 4 minutes more.
5. add cilantro, stir, cook for 1 minute and take off heat.
6. divide zucchini noodles into soup bowls, add soup on top and serve with lime wedges on the side.

Nutrition Per Serving: calories 287, fat 14, fiber 2, carbs 7, protein 25

Delicious lunch curry

Preparation time: 10 minutes cooking time: 1 hour servings: 4

Ingredients:

- 3 tomatoes, chopped
- 2 tablespoons olive oil
- 1 cup chicken stock
- 14 ounces canned coconut milk
- 1 tablespoon lime juice
- Salt and black pepper to the taste
- 2 pounds chicken thighs, boneless and skinless and cubed
- 2 garlic cloves, minced
- 1 cup white onion, chopped

- 3 red chilies, chopped
- 1 ounce peanuts, toasted
- 1 tablespoon water
- 1 tablespoon ginger, grated
- 2 teaspoons coriander, ground
- 1 teaspoon cinnamon, ground
- 1 teaspoon turmeric, ground
- 1 teaspoon cumin, ground
- ½ teaspoon black pepper
- 1 teaspoon fennel seeds, ground

Directions:

1. In your food processor, mix white onion with garlic, peanuts, red chilies, water, ginger, coriander, cinnamon, turmeric, cumin, fennel and black pepper, blend until you obtain a paste and leave aside for now.
2. heat up a pan with the olive oil over medium high heat, add spice paste you've made, stir well and heat up for a few seconds.
3. add chicken pieces, stir and cook for 2 minutes.
4. add stock and tomatoes, stir, reduce heat to low and cook for minutes.
5. add coconut milk, stir and cook for 20 minutes more.
6. add salt, pepper and lime juice, stir, divide into bowls and serve.

Nutrition Per Serving: calories 430, fat 22, fiber 4, carbs 7, protein 53

Lunch spinach rolls

Preparation time: 20 minutes cooking time: 15 minutes servings: 16

Ingredients:

- 6 tablespoons coconut flour
- ½ cup almond flour
- 2 and ½ cups mozzarella cheese, shredded

- 2 eggs
- A pinch of salt
- For the filling:
- 4 ounces cream cheese

- 6 ounces spinach, torn
- A drizzle of avocado oil
- A pinch of salt
- ¼ cup parmesan, grated
- Mayonnaise for serving

Directions:

1. heat up a pan with the oil over medium heat, add spinach and cook for 2 minutes.
2. add parmesan, a pinch of salt and cream cheese, stir well, take off heat and leave aside for now.
3. put mozzarella cheese in a heatproof bowl and microwave for 30 seconds.
4. add eggs, salt, coconut and almond flour and stir everything.
5. place dough on a lined cutting board, place a parchment paper on top and flatten dough with a rolling pin.
6. divide dough into 16 rectangles, spread spinach mix on each and roll them into cigar shapes.
7. place all rolls on a lined baking sheet, introduce in the oven at 350 degrees f and bake for 15 minutes.
8. leave rolls to cool down for a few minutes before serving them with some mayo on top.
9. Enjoy!

Nutrition Per Serving: calories 500, fat 65, fiber 4, carbs 14, protein 32

Delicious steak bowl

Preparation time: 15 minutes cooking time: 8 minutes servings: 4

Ingredients:

- 16 ounces skirt steak
- 4 ounces pepper jack cheese, shredded
- 1 cup sour cream
- Salt and black pepper to the taste
- 1 handful cilantro, chopped
- A splash of chipotle adobo sauce
- For the guacamole:
- ¼ cup red onion, chopped
- 2 avocados, pitted and peeled
- Juice from 1 lime
- 1 tablespoon olive oil
- 6 cherry tomatoes, chopped
- 1 garlic clove, minced
- 1 tablespoon cilantro, chopped
- Salt and black pepper to the taste

Directions:

1. put avocados in a bowl and mash with a fork.
2. add tomatoes, red onion, garlic, salt and pepper and stir well.

3. add olive oil, lime juice and 1 tablespoon cilantro, stir again very well and leave aside for now.
4. heat up a pan over high heat, add steak, season with salt and pepper, cook for 4 minutes on each side, transfer to a cutting board, leave aside to cool down a bit and cut into thin strips.
5. divide steak into 4 bowls, add cheese, sour cream and guacamole on top and serve with a splash of chipotle adobo sauce.
6. Enjoy!

Nutrition Per Serving: calories 600, fat 50, fiber 6, carbs 5, protein 30

Meatballs and pilaf

Preparation time: 10 minutes cooking time: 30 minutes servings: 4

Ingredients:

- 12 ounces cauliflower florets
- Salt and black pepper to the taste
- 1 egg
- 1 pound lamb, ground
- 1 teaspoon fennel seed
- 1 teaspoon paprika
- 1 teaspoon garlic powder
- 1 small yellow onion, chopped
- 2 garlic cloves, minced
- 2 tablespoons coconut oil
- 1 bunch mint, chopped
- 1 tablespoon lemon zest
- 4 ounces goat cheese, crumbled

Directions:

1. put cauliflower florets in your food processor, add salt and pulse well.
2. grease a pan with some of the coconut oil, heat up over medium heat, add cauliflower rice, cook for 8 minutes, season with salt and pepper to the taste, take off heat and keep warm.
3. in a bowl, mix lamb with salt, pepper, egg, paprika, garlic powder and fennel seed and stir very well.
4. shape 12 meatballs and place them on a plate for now.
5. heat up a pan with the coconut oil over medium heat, add onion, stir and cook for 6 minutes.
6. add garlic, stir and cook for 1 minute.
7. add meatballs, cook them well on all sides and take off heat.
8. divide cauliflower rice between plates, add meatballs and onion mix on top, sprinkle mint, lemon zest and goat cheese at the end and serve.

Nutrition Per Serving: calories 470, fat 43, fiber 5, carbs 4, protein 26

Delicious broccoli soup

Preparation time: 10 minutes cooking time: 30 minutes servings: 4

Ingredients:

- 1 white onion, chopped
- 1 tablespoon ghee
- 2 cups veggie stock
- Salt and black pepper to the taste
- 2 cups water
- 2 garlic cloves, minced
- 1 cup heavy cream
- 8 ounces cheddar cheese, grated
- 12 ounces broccoli florets
- ½ teaspoon paprika

Directions:

1. heat up a pot with the ghee over medium heat, add onion and garlic, stir and cook for 5 minutes.
2. add stock, cream, water, salt, pepper and paprika, stir and bring to a boil.
3. add broccoli, stir and simmer soup for 25 minutes.
4. transfer to your food processor and blend well.
5. add cheese and blend again.
6. divide into soup bowls and serve hot.
7. Enjoy!

Nutrition Per Serving: calories 350, fat 34, fiber 7, carbs 7, protein 11

Lunch green beans salad

Preparation time: 10 minutes cooking time: 5 minutes servings: 8

Ingredients:

- 2 tablespoons white wine vinegar
- 1 and ½ tablespoons mustard
- Salt and black pepper to the taste
- 2 pounds green beans
- 1/3 cup extra virgin olive oil
- 1 and ½ cups fennel, thinly sliced
- 4 ounces goat cheese, crumbled

- ¾ cup walnuts, toasted and chopped

Directions:

1. put water in a pot, add some salt and bring to a boil over medium high heat.
2. add green beans, cook for 5 minutes and transfer them to a bowl filled with ice water.
3. drain green beans well and put them in a salad bowl.
4. add walnuts, fennel and goat cheese and toss gently.
5. in a bowl, mix vinegar with mustard, salt, pepper and oil and whisk well.
6. pour this over salad, toss to coat well and serve for lunch.
7. Enjoy!

Nutrition Per Serving: calories 200, fat 14, fiber 4, carbs 5, protein 6

Pumpkin soup

Preparation time: 10 minutes cooking time: 20 minutes servings: 6

Ingredients:

- ½ cup yellow onion, chopped
- 2 tablespoons olive oil
- 1 tablespoon chipotles in adobo sauce
- 1 garlic clove, minced
- 1 teaspoon cumin, ground
- 1 teaspoon coriander, ground
- A pinch of allspice
- 2 cups pumpkin puree
- Salt and black pepper to the taste
- 32 ounces chicken stock
- ½ cup heavy cream
- 2 teaspoons vinegar
- 2 teaspoons stevia

Directions:

1. heat up a pot with the oil over medium heat, add onions and garlic, stir and cook for 4 minutes.
2. add stevia, cumin, coriander, chipotles and cumin, stir and cook for 2 minutes.
3. add stock and pumpkin puree, stir and cook for 5 minutes.
4. blend soup well using an immersion blender and then mix with salt, pepper, heavy cream and vinegar.
5. stir, cook for 5 minutes more and divide into bowls.
6. serve right away.
7. Enjoy!

Nutrition Per Serving: calories 140, fat 12, fiber 3, carbs 6, protein 2

Delicious green beans casserole

Preparation time: 10 minutes cooking time: 35 minutes servings: 8

Ingredients:

- 1-pound green beans, halved
- Salt and black pepper to the taste
- ½ cup almond flour
- 2 tablespoons ghee
- 8 ounces mushrooms, chopped
- 4 ounces onion, chopped
- 2 shallots, chopped
- 3 garlic cloves, minced
- ½ cup chicken stock
- ½ cup heavy cream
- ¼ cup parmesan, grated
- Avocado oil for frying

Directions:

1. put some water in a pot, add salt, bring to a boil over medium high heat, add green beans, cook for 5 minutes, transfer to a bowl filled with ice water, cool down, drain well and leave aside for now.
2. in a bowl, mix shallots with onions, almond flour, salt and pepper and toss to coat.
3. heat up a pan with some avocado oil over medium high heat, add onions and shallots mix, fry until they are golden.
4. transfer to paper towels and drain grease.
5. heat up the same pan over medium heat, add ghee and melt it.
6. add garlic and mushrooms, stir and cook for 5 minutes. add stock and heavy cream, stir, bring to a boil and simmer until it thickens.
7. add parmesan and green beans, toss to coat and take off heat.
8. transfer this mix to a baking dish, sprinkle crispy onions mix all over, introduce in the oven at 400 degrees f and bake for 15 minutes.

Nutrition Per Serving: calories 155, fat, 11, fiber 6, carbs 8, protein 5

Simple lunch apple salad

Preparation time: 10 minutes cooking time: 0 minutes servings: 4

Ingredients:

- 2 cups broccoli florets, roughly chopped
- 2 ounces pecans, chopped
- 1 apple, cored and grated
- 1 green onion stalk, finely chopped
- Salt and black pepper to the taste
- 2 teaspoons poppy seeds
- 1 teaspoon apple cider vinegar
- ¼ cup mayonnaise
- ½ teaspoon lemon juice
- ¼ cup sour cream

Directions:

1. in a salad bowl, mix apple with broccoli, green onion and pecans and stir.
2. add poppy seeds, salt and pepper and toss gently.
3. in a bowl, mix mayo with sour cream, vinegar and lemon juice and whisk well.
4. pour this over salad, toss to coat well and serve cold for lunch!
5. Enjoy!

Nutrition Per Serving: calories 250, fat 23, fiber 4, carbs 4, protein 5

Brussels sprouts gratin

Preparation time: 10 minutes cooking time: 35 minutes servings: 4

Ingredients:

- 2 ounces onions, chopped
- 1 teaspoon garlic, minced
- 6 ounces brussels sprouts, chopped
- 2 tablespoons ghee
- 1 tablespoon coconut aminos
- Salt and black pepper to the taste
- ½ teaspoon liquid smoke
- For the sauce:
- 2.5 ounces cheddar cheese, grated
- A pinch of black pepper
- 1 tablespoon ghee
- ½ cup heavy cream
- ¼ teaspoon turmeric
- ¼ teaspoon paprika
- A pinch of xanthan gum
- For the pork crust:
- 3 tablespoons parmesan
- 0.5 ounces pork rinds
- ½ teaspoon sweet paprika

Directions:

1. heat up a pan with 2 tablespoons ghee over high heat, add brussels sprouts, salt and pepper, stir and cook for 3 minutes.
2. add garlic and onion, stir and cook for 3 minutes more.
3. add liquid smoke and coconut aminos, stir, take off heat and leave aside for now.

4. heat up another pan with 1 tablespoon ghee over medium heat, add heavy cream and stir.
5. add cheese, black pepper, turmeric, paprika and xanthan gum, stir and cook until it thickens again.
6. add brussels sprouts mix, toss to coat and divide into ramekins.
7. in your food processor, mix parmesan with pork rinds and ½ Teaspoon paprika and pulse well.
8. divide these crumbs on top of brussels sprouts mix, introduce ramekins in the oven at 375 degrees f and bake for 20 minutes.
9. serve right away.
10. Enjoy!

Nutrition Per Serving: calories 300, fat 20, fiber 6, carbs 5, protein 10

Simple asparagus lunch

Preparation time: 10 minutes cooking time: 10 minutes servings: 4

Ingredients:

- 2 egg yolks
- Salt and black pepper to the taste
- ¼ cup ghee
- 1 tablespoon lemon juice
- A pinch of cayenne pepper
- 40 asparagus spears

Directions:

1. in a bowl, whisk egg yolks very well.
2. transfer this to a small pan over low heat.
3. add lemon juice and whisk well.
4. add ghee and whisk until it melts.
5. add salt, pepper and cayenne pepper and whisk again well.
6. meanwhile, heat up a pan over medium high heat, add asparagus spears and fry them for 5 minutes.
7. divide asparagus on plates, drizzle the sauce you've made on top and serve.
8. Enjoy!

Nutrition Per Serving: calories 150, fat 13, fiber 6, carbs 2, protein 3

Simple shrimp pasta

Preparation time: 10 minutes cooking time: 10 minutes servings: 4

Ingredients:

- 12 ounces angel hair noodles
- 2 tablespoons olive oil
- Salt and black pepper to the taste
- 2 tablespoons ghee
- 4 garlic cloves, minced
- 1 pound shrimp, raw, peeled and deveined
- Juice of ½ lemon
- ½ teaspoon paprika
- A handful basil, chopped

Directions:

1. put water in a pot, add some salt, bring to a boil, add noodles, cook for 2 minutes, drain them and transfer to a heated pan.
2. toast noodles for a few seconds, take off heat and leave them aside.
3. heat up a pan with the ghee and olive oil over medium heat, add garlic, stir and brown for 1 minute.
4. add shrimp and lemon juice and cook for 3 minutes on each side.
5. add noodles, salt, pepper and paprika, stir, divide into bowls and serve with chopped basil on top.
6. Enjoy!

Nutrition Per Serving: calories 300, fat 20, fiber 6, carbs 3, protein 30

Shrimp Scampi Spinach Salad

Preparation time: 10 minutes Cooking time: 10 minutes Servings: 4

Ingredients:

- Two tablespoons butter
- 1-pound uncooked shrimp
- Three garlic cloves, minced
- Two tablespoons chopped fresh parsley
- 6 ounces fresh baby spinach (about 8 cups)
- 1 cup cherry tomatoes, halved
- Lemon halves
- 1/8 teaspoon salt
- 1/8 teaspoon coarsely ground pepper
- 1/4 cup sliced almonds, toasted
- Shredded Parmesan cheese, optional

Instructions:

1. In a large skillet, heat butter over medium heat; saute shrimp and garlic until shrimp turn pink, 3-4 minutes. Stir in parsley; remove from heat.
2. To serve, place spinach and tomatoes in a serving dish; top with shrimp mixture. Squeeze lemon juice over salad; sprinkle with salt and pepper. Sprinkle with almonds and, if desired, cheese.

Nutrition Per Serving: 201 calories,10g fat,153mg cholesterol,291mg sodium,21g protein

Almighty Almond Cheesecake

Preparation time: 5 minutes Cooking time: 20 minutes Servings: 4

Ingredients:
- 24 oz cream cheese.
- Four large eggs.
- 1 cup stevia.
- ⅓ cup sour cream.
- ½ tsp almond extract.

Instructions:
1. Preheat the oven at 175 degrees.
2. In a bowl, whisk the cream cheese until smooth, then gently add in stevia, sour cream, and almond extract, mix until well combined.
3. Add the eggs one by one and whisk until a thick, creamy mixture is formed.
4. Grease a springform pan, pour in the mixture, and bake for 45-50 minutes until puffed and lightly browned.

5. Remove from the oven and allow to sit at room temperature for an hour.
6. Place in the refrigerator for 5-6 hours.

Nutrition Per Serving: Fat: 29g, Carbohydrates: 3g, Protein: 8g, Calories: 281

Zesty Orange Ice Cream

Preparation time: 5 minutes Cooking time: 10 minutes Servings: 4

Ingredients:

- 2 large eggs (separated).
- One ¼ cups thick whipping cream.
- 2 tbsp erythritol (powder).
- ½ tsp orange extract.

Instructions:

1. In a bowl, whisk the egg yolks until smooth.
2. In a saucepan, mix the whipping cream, erythritol, and orange extract. Bring to the boil then simmer until slightly thickened.
3. Reduce the heat to low and stir in the whisked egg yolks. Simmer gently until the mixture thickens, stirring continuously.
4. Place in the fridge until cold.
5. In a bowl, whisk the egg whites until soft peaks are formed.
6. Fold the egg whites into the cooled cream mixture.
7. Pour into a container and seal the lid tightly; freeze for 3-4 hours.

Nutrition Per Serving: Fat: 61g, Carbohydrates: 5g, Protein: 13g, Calories: 590

Zingy Lemon & Lime Pancakes

Preparation time: 5 minutes Cooking time: 20 minutes Servings: 4

Ingredients:

- 4 eggs.
- 2 cups almond flour.
- ¼ cup of water.
- 8 tbsp butter (melted).
- 2 tbsp swerve.
- 1 tbsp coconut oil.
- 1 tsp baking powder.
- One lime zest
- One lemon zest.

Instructions:

1. Place all ingredients in a blender and blend until well combined.
2. Allow resting for 10-15 minutes.
3. In a frying pan, heat a little oil, pour in ⅓ cup of the butter mixture.
4. Cook for 2-3 minutes on each side until golden brown.
5. Repeat the process until all of the batters have gone.

Nutrition Per Serving: Fat: 28g, Carbohydrates: 4g, Protein: 9g, Calories: 273

Mushroom Leek Sauce

Preparation time: 5 minutes Cooking time: 10 minutes Servings: 4

Ingredients:

- One beef top sirloin steak (1-1/4 pounds)
- Two tablespoons Cajun seasoning
- Two tablespoons olive oil
- 1/2 pound sliced assorted fresh mushrooms
- One medium leek (white portion only), halved and sliced
- One tablespoon butter
- One teaspoon minced garlic
- 1-1/2 cups dry red wine or reduced-sodium beef broth
- 1/4 teaspoon pepper
- 1/8 teaspoon salt

Instructions:

1. Rub steak with Cajun seasoning; let stand for 5 minutes.
2. In a large skillet, cook steak in oil over medium-high heat for 7-10 minutes on each side or until meat reaches desired doneness (for medium-rare, a thermometer should read 135°; medium, 140°; medium-well, 145°). Remove and keep warm.

3. In the same skillet, saute mushrooms and leek in butter until tender. Add garlic; cook 1 minute longer. Add the wine, pepper, and salt, stirring to loosen browned bits from pan. Bring to a boil; cook until liquid is reduced by half. Slice steak; serve with mushroom sauce.

Nutrition Per Serving: 325 calories,16g fat,65mg cholesterol,976mg sodium,32g protein.

Sage-Rubbed Salmon

Preparation time: 10 minutes Cooking time: 15 minutes Servings: 2

Ingredients

- Two tablespoons minced fresh sage
- One teaspoon garlic powder
- One teaspoon kosher salt
- One teaspoon freshly ground pepper
- One skin-on salmon fillet (1-1/2 pounds)
- Two tablespoons olive oil

Instructions:

1. Preheat oven to 375°. Mix the first four ingredients; rub onto the flesh side of salmon. Cut into six portions.
2. In a large cast-iron skillet, heat oil over medium heat. Add salmon, skin side down; cook 5 minutes. Transfer skillet to oven; bake just until fish flakes easily with a fork, about 10 minutes.

Nutrition Per Serving: 220 calories, 15g fat, 57mg cholesterol,377mg sodium,19g protein.

Chicken Provolone

Preparation time: 10 minutes Cooking time: 15 minutes Servings: 4

Ingredients

- Four boneless skinless chicken breast halves (4 ounces each)
- 1/4 teaspoon pepper
- Eight fresh basil leaves
- Butter-flavoured cooking spray
- Four thin slices prosciutto or deli ham
- 4 slices provolone cheese

Instructions:

1. Sprinkle chicken with pepper. In a large skillet coated with cooking spray, cook chicken over medium heat until a thermometer reads 165°, 4-5 minutes on each side.
2. Transfer to an ungreased baking sheet; top with the basil, prosciutto, and cheese. Broil 6-8 in. From the heat until cheese is melted, 1-2 minutes.

Nutrition Per Serving: 236 calories,11 g fat,89 mg of cholesterol,435 mg sodium,33mg protein.

Lemon-Pepper Tilapia with Mushrooms

Preparation time: 5 minutes Cooking time: 15 minutes Servings: 4

Ingredients:

- Two tablespoons butter
- 1/2 pound sliced fresh mushrooms
- 3/4 teaspoon lemon-pepper seasoning, divided
- Three garlic cloves, minced
- Four tilapia fillets (6 ounces each)
- 1/4 teaspoon paprika
- 1/8 teaspoon cayenne pepper
- One medium tomato, chopped
- Three green onions, thinly sliced

Instructions:

1. In a 12-in. Skillet, heat butter over medium heat. Add mushrooms and 1/4 teaspoon lemon pepper; cook and stir 3-5 minutes or until tender. Add garlic; cook 30 seconds longer.
2. Place fillets over mushrooms; sprinkle with paprika, cayenne, and remaining lemon pepper. Cook, covered, 5-7 minutes or until fish just begins to flake easily with a fork. Top with tomato and green onions.

Nutrition Per Serving: 216 calories,8g fat,98mg cholesterol,173mg sodium,34g protein,

Cheese & Herb Balls

Preparation time: 10 minutes Cooking time: 20 minutes Servings: 5

Ingredients:

- 5 oz cheddar cheese (grated).
- 5 oz cream cheese.
- 5 oz bacon.
- 2 oz butter.
- ½ tsp chilli flakes.
- ½ tsp black pepper.
- ½ tsp Italian seasoning.

Instructions:

1. Heat the butter in a large frying pan and fry the bacon until crispy. Reserve bacon fat and chop the bacon into small pieces.
2. In a bowl, mix cream cheese, cheddar cheese, chilli flakes, pepper, Italian seasoning, and bacon fat until well combined.
3. Place the cream cheese mix in the fridge for 20 minutes.
4. When the mixture is set, roll 24 balls into shape.
5. Roll each ball in the bacon pieces before serving.

Nutrition Per Serving: Fat: 29g, Carbohydrates: 2g, Protein: 9g, Calories: 273

Smoked Salmon Lettuce Wrap

Preparation time: 5 minutes Cooking time: 20 minutes Servings: 4

Ingredients:
- 8 oz cream cheese
- 7 oz smoked salmon (canned and drained).
- 2 oz iceberg lettuce leaves.
- 5 tbsp mayonnaise.
- 4 tbsp chives (finely chopped).
- ½ lemon zest.

Instructions:
1. In a large bowl, mix everything (except lettuce leaves) together until well combined.
2. Place in the refrigerator for 15-20 minutes.
3. When chilled, scoop onto lettuce leaves and serve.

Nutrition Per Serving: Fat: 24g, Carbohydrates: 3g, Protein: 10g, Calories: 263

Creamy Zucchini Noodles

Preparation time: 10 minutes Cooking time: 20 minutes Servings: 4

Ingredients:
- 32 oz zucchini.
- 10 oz bacon (diced).
- One ¼ cups thick cream.
- ¼ cup mayonnaise.
- 3 oz parmesan (grated).
- 1 tbsp butter.

Instructions:
1. Heat the cream in a large saucepan; bring to a gentle boil and allow to reduce slightly.
2. Heat the butter in a large frying pan and cook the bacon until crispy; set aside and leave grease warming in the pan (low heat).
3. Add the mayonnaise to the cream and turn down the heat.
4. Using a potato peeler, make thin zucchini strips—Cook the zucchini noodles for 30 seconds in a pan of boiling water.
5. Add cream mixture and bacon fat to the zucchini noodles, tossing to ensure all are coated. Mix in the bacon and parmesan

Nutrition Per Serving: Fat: 78g, Carbohydrates: 8g, Protein: 21g, Calories: 801

Creamy Dijon Chicken

Preparation time: 10 minutes Cooking time: 15 minutes Servings: 4

Ingredients:

- 1/2 cup half-and-half cream
- 1/4 cup Dijon mustard
- One tablespoon brown sugar
- Four boneless skinless chicken breast halves
- 1/4 teaspoon salt
- 1/4 teaspoon pepper
- Two teaspoons olive oil
- Two teaspoons butter
- One small onion halved and very thinly sliced
- Minced fresh parsley

Instructions:

1. Whisk together cream, mustard, and brown sugar. Pound chicken breasts with a meat mallet to even thickness; sprinkle with salt and pepper.
2. In a large skillet, heat oil and butter over medium-high heat; brown chicken on both sides. Reduce heat to medium. Add onion and cream mixture; bring to a boil. Reduce heat; simmer, covered, until a thermometer inserted in chicken reads 165°, 10-12 minutes. Sprinkle with parsley.

Nutrition Per Serving: 295 calories,11g fat, 114mg cholesterol,621mg sodium, 36g protein.

Mom's Roast Chicken

Preparation time: 5 minutes Cooking time: 15 minutes Servings: 6

Ingredients:

- One broiler/fryer chicken (4 to 5 pounds)
- Two teaspoons kosher salt
- One teaspoon coarsely ground pepper
- Two teaspoons olive oil
- Minced fresh thyme or rosemary, optional

Instructions:

1. Rub outside of the chicken with salt and pepper. Transfer chicken to a rack on a rimmed baking sheet. Refrigerate, uncovered, overnight.

2. Preheat oven to 450°. Remove chicken from refrigerator while oven heats. Heat a 12-in. Cast-iron or ovenproof skillet in the oven for 15 minutes.
3. Place chicken on a work surface, neck side down. Cut through the skin where legs connect to the body. Press thighs down so joints pop and legs lie flat.
4. Carefully place chicken, breast side up, into hot skillet; press legs down so they lie flat on the bottom of the pan. Brush with oil. Roast until a thermometer inserted in the thickest part of the thigh reads 170°-175°, 35-40 minutes. Remove chicken from oven; let stand 10 minutes before carving. If desired, top with herbs before serving.

Nutrition Per Serving: 405 calories,24g fat, 139mg cholesterol,760mg sodium,44g protein.

Cod and Asparagus Bake

Preparation time: 10 minutes Cooking time: 15 minutes Servings: 4

Ingredients:

- Four cod fillets (4 ounces each)
- 1-pound fresh thin asparagus, trimmed
- 1-pint cherry tomatoes halved
- Two tablespoons lemon juice
- 1-1/2 teaspoons grated lemon zest
- 1/4 cup grated Romano cheese

Instructions:

1. Preheat oven to 375°. Place cod and asparagus in a 15x10x1-in. Baking pan brushed with oil. Add tomatoes, cut sides down. Brush fish with lemon juice; sprinkle with lemon zest. Sprinkle fish and vegetables with Romano cheese. Bake until fish just begins to flake easily with a fork, about 12 minutes.
2. Remove pan from oven; preheat broiler. Broil cod mixture 3-4 in. From heat until vegetables are lightly browned, 2-3 minutes.

Nutrition Per Serving: 141 calories,3g fat, 45mg cholesterol,184mg sodium,6g carbohydrate,23g protein,

Parmesan Chicken

Preparation time: 10 minutes Cooking time: 15 minutes Servings: 4

Ingredients:

- 1/2 cup butter, melted
- Two teaspoons Dijon mustard
- One teaspoon Worcestershire sauce
- 1/2 teaspoon salt
- 1 cup dry bread crumbs
- 1/2 cup grated Parmesan cheese
- Six boneless skinless chicken breast halves (7 ounces each)

Instructions:

1. Preheat oven to 350°. In a shallow bowl, combine butter, mustard, Worcestershire sauce, and salt. Place bread crumbs and cheese in another shallow dish. Dip chicken in butter mixture, then in bread crumb mixture, patting to help coating adhere.
2. Place in an ungreased 15x10x1-in. Baking pan. Drizzle with any remaining butter mixture. Bake, uncovered, until a thermometer inserted in chicken reads 165°, 25-30 minutes.

Nutrition Per Serving: 270 calories,16g fat,82mg cholesterol,552mg sodium,10g carbohydrate,21g protein.

Tuna & Cheese Oven Bake

Preparation time: 5 minutes Cooking time: 20 minutes Servings: 4

Ingredients:

- 16 oz tuna (tinned in olive oil).
- 5 oz celery (finely chopped).
- 4 oz parmesan (grated).
- 1 cup mayonnaise.
- One green bell pepper (diced).
- One onion (diced).
- 2 oz butter.
- 1 tsp chilli flakes.

Instructions:

1. Preheat the oven at 200 degrees.
2. In a large frying pan, fry the celery, pepper, and onion until soft.
3. In a bowl, mix tuna, mayonnaise, parmesan, and chilli flakes until well combined.
4. Stir in the cooked vegetables; pour the mixture into an ovenproof dish.
5. Bake for 15-20 minutes or until golden brown.

Nutrition Per Serving: Fat: 85g, Carbohydrates: 5g, Protein: 44g, Calories: 957

Tomato & Leek Bake

Preparation time: 10 minutes Cooking time: 20 minutes Servings: 4

Ingredients:

- 12 large eggs.
- One cup of thick cream.
- ½ leek (thinly sliced).
- 7 oz cheddar cheese (grated).
- 3 oz cherry tomatoes (halved).
- 1 oz parmesan (grated).
- 1 tsp onion powder.
- ½ tsp black pepper.

Instructions:

1. Preheat the oven at 200 degrees.
2. Grease a large ovenproof dish and sprinkle in the diced leeks.
3. In a large bowl, whisk together eggs, cheddar cheese, onion powder, and black pepper.
4. Pour the egg mixture over the leeks; add cherry tomatoes and parmesan to the top.
5. Bake for 40-45 minutes until completely set.

Nutrition Per Serving: Fat: 51g, Carbohydrates: 5g, Protein: 34g, Calories: 627

Spicy Crab Pot Pie

Preparation time: 5 minutes Cooking time: 15 minutes Servings: 4

Ingredients:

- 4 large eggs (lightly whisked).
- 16 oz of crab meat (tinned & drained).
- 12 oz cheddar cheese (grated).
- 1 cup mayonnaise.
- One red onion (diced).
- 2 tbsp butter.
- 2 tsp paprika.
- ¼ tsp cayenne pepper.

Instructions:

1. Preheat the oven 180 degrees.
2. Heat the butter and fry the onion until tender.
3. In a large bowl, mix eggs, mayonnaise, crab, paprika, cayenne pepper, and ⅔ cheddar cheese; stir in the fried onions.
4. Pour the mixture into a greased ovenproof dish, sprinkle over the remaining cheddar cheese.
5. Bake for 30-35 minutes until firm and golden brown.

Nutrition Per Serving: Fat: 99g, Carbohydrates: 6g, Protein: 50g, Calories: 1106

Bed of Baby Spinach

Preparation time: 5 minutes Cooking time: 15 minutes Servings: 4

Ingredients:

- 16 oz tinned tuna (drained).
- 8 oz baby spinach.
- Two onions (finely diced).
- One large egg.
- ¼ cup mayonnaise.
- ⅓ cup almond flour.
- 2 tbsp fresh dill (finely chopped).
- 1 tbsp lemon zest.
- 1 tbsp olive oil.
- 2 tbsp avocado oil.

Instructions:

1. In a large bowl, mix tuna, onions, egg, mayonnaise, almond flour, dill, and lemon zest.
2. From the mixture, form 8 burgers.
3. Heat 1 tbsp avocado oil in a large frying pan, fry four tuna patties for 4-5 minutes, flip and cook for an additional 4 minutes. Repeat with remaining oil and burgers.
4. Place the spinach on a serving plate and drizzle with olive oil, top with burgers.

Nutrition Per Serving: Fat: 16g, Carbohydrates: 2g, Protein: 21g, Calories: 217

Salmon & Spinach Casserole

Preparation time: 5 minutes Cooking time: 20 minutes Servings: 4

Ingredients:

- 10 oz tinned salmon.
- 9 oz spinach (frozen).
- 1 ½ cups parmesan (grated).
- One cup of thick cream.
- ½ cup of almond milk.
- ¼ cup butter.
- Four slices mozzarella.
- One garlic clove (crushed).
- 1 tbsp parsley (dried).

Instructions:

1. Preheat the oven at 180 degrees.
2. In a large saucepan, heat the butter with the garlic. When garlic is browned, add in almond milk and cream.
3. Heat for 5-6 minutes and stir in parmesan, spinach, parsley, and salmon.
4. Continuously stir until the mixture is bubbling...
5. Pour into an ovenproof dish and top with mozzarella cheese.
6. Bake for 25-30 minutes until bubbling and golden.

Nutrition Per Serving: Fat: 54g, Carbohydrates: 5g, Protein: 37g, Calories: 640

California Burger Wraps

Preparation time: 15 minutes Cooking time: 25 minutes Servings: 4

Ingredients:

- 1-pound lean ground beef (90% lean)
- 1/2 teaspoon salt
- 1/4 teaspoon pepper
- 8 Bibb lettuce leaves
- 1/3 cup crumbled feta cheese
- Two tablespoons Miracle Whip Light
- 1/2 medium ripe avocado, peeled and cut into eight slices
- 1/4 cup chopped red onion
- Chopped cherry tomatoes, optional

Instructions:

1. In a large bowl, combine beef, salt, and pepper, mixing lightly but thoroughly. Shape into eight 1/2-in.-thick patties.
2. Grill burgers, covered, over medium heat or broil 3-4 in. From heat until a thermometer reads 160°, 3-4 minutes on each side. Place burgers in lettuce leaves. Combine feta and Miracle Whip; spread over burgers. Top with avocado, red onion, and if desired, tomatoes.

Nutrition Per Serving: 252 calories,15g fat,78mg cholesterol,518mg sodium,24g protein.

Blue Cheese Pork Medallions

Preparation time: 10 minutes Cooking time: 15 minutes Servings: 4

Ingredients:

- One pork tenderloin (1 pound)
- Two teaspoons Montreal steak seasoning
- Two tablespoons butter
- 1/2 cup heavy whipping cream
- 1/4 cup crumbled blue cheese
- One tablespoon minced fresh parsley

Instructions:

1. Cut pork into 12 slices; sprinkle with steak seasoning. In a large skillet, heat butter over medium heat. Add pork; cook, covered, until pork is tender, 3-5 minutes per side. Remove from pan; keep warm.
2. Add cream to skillet; bring to a boil, stirring to loosen browned bits from pan. Cook until the cream is slightly thickened, 2-3 minutes. Stir in cheese until melted. Serve with pork. Sprinkle with parsley.

Nutrition Per Serving: 317 calories,23g fat,126mg cholesterol,539mg sodium, 25g protein.

Chicken Nicoise Salad

Preparation time: 10 minutes Cooking time: 10 minutes Servings: 2

Ingredients:

- 1/2-pound fresh green beans, trimmed and halved (about 1 cup)
- DRESSING:
- 1/4 cup olive oil
- Two teaspoons grated lemon zest
- Two tablespoons lemon juice
- Two garlic cloves, minced
- One teaspoon Dijon mustard
- 1/8 teaspoon salt
- Dash pepper

SALAD:

- One can (5 ounces) light tuna in water, drained and flaked
- Two tablespoons sliced ripe olives, drained
- One teaspoon caper, rinsed and drained
- 2 cups torn mixed salad greens
- One package (6 ounces) ready-to-use Southwest-style grilled chicken breast strips
- One small red onion halved and thinly sliced
- One medium sweet red pepper, julienned
- Two large hard-boiled eggs, cut into wedges

Instructions:

1. In a saucepan, cook green beans in boiling water just until crisp-tender. Remove and immediately drop into ice water to cool. Drain; pat dry.
2. Meanwhile, whisk together dressing ingredients. In a small bowl, lightly toss tuna with olives and capers.

3. Line platter with salad greens; top with tuna mixture, green beans, and remaining ingredients. Serve with dressing.

Nutrition Per Serving: 289 calories,18g fat,142mg cholesterol,562mg sodium,24g protein.

Cauliflower & Ham Bake

Preparation time: 10 minutes Cooking time: 15 minutes Servings: 4

Ingredients:

- 2 large eggs.
- Two garlic cloves (crushed).
- ⅔ cup of almond milk (unsweetened).
- ½ cup of dry white wine.
- ½ cup cheddar cheese (grated).
- ½ cup mozzarella (grated).
- 10 oz spinach (frozen & defrosted).
- 8 oz cooked ham.
- 1 tbsp olive oil.

Instructions:
1. Preheat the oven at 190 degrees.
2. In a large bowl, mix spinach, cauliflower rice, milk, eggs, ⅓ cup mozzarella, and ⅓ cup cheddar.
3. In a large frying pan, heat the olive oil and fry the garlic until lightly browned. Stir in the white wine and cook until wine evaporates; add the ham and cook for 2-3 minutes.
4. Combine the ham mixture to the spinach mixture.
5. Add mixture to an ovenproof dish, sprinkle the remaining cheese on top.
6. Bake for 30-35 minutes until golden brown.

Nutrition Per Serving: Fat: 17g, Carbohydrates: 7g, Protein: 19g, Calories: 284

Green Bean & Garlic Bacon Crumble

Preparation time: 5 minutes Cooking time: 15 minutes Servings: 4

Ingredients:
- 16 oz green beans (trimmed).
- Six garlic cloves (crushed).
- Six bacon rashers.
- 1 tbsp olive oil.
- 1 tbsp butter.
- ½ tsp salt.

Instructions:

1. In a large frying pan, fry the bacon until crispy and set aside.
2. Bring a large saucepan of water to the boil, add green beans and salt and cook for 5-7 minutes; drain and set aside.
3. In the same frying pan where the bacon was cooked, melt butter and olive oil, fry the garlic for 30 seconds until lightly browned. Crumble in the cooked, crispy bacon and add the green beans to the pan; saute for 1-2 minutes, stirring continuously.

Nutrition Per Serving: Fat: 21g, Carbohydrates: 7g, Protein: 9g, Calories: 239

Haddock with Lime-Cilantro Butter

Preparation time: 5 minutes Cooking time: 15 minutes Servings: 4

.

Ingredients:

- Four haddock fillets (6 ounces each)
- 1/2 teaspoon salt
- 1/4 teaspoon pepper
- Three tablespoons butter, melted
- Two tablespoons minced fresh cilantro
- One tablespoon lime juice
- One teaspoon grated lime zest

Instructions:

1. Preheat broiler. Sprinkle fillets with salt and pepper. Place on a greased broiler pan. Broil 4-5 in. From heat until fish flakes easily with a fork, 5-6 minutes.
2. In a small bowl, mix the remaining ingredients. Serve over fish.

Nutrition Per Serving: 227 calories,10g fat,121mg cholesterol,479mg sodium,1g carbohydrate, 32g protein.

Shakshuka

Preparation time: 5 minutes Cooking time: 15 minutes Servings: 4

Ingredients:

- Two tablespoons olive oil
- One medium onion, chopped
- One garlic clove, minced
- One teaspoon ground cumin
- One teaspoon pepper
- 1/2 to 1 teaspoon chilli powder
- 1/2 teaspoon salt

- One teaspoon Sriracha chilli sauce or hot pepper sauce, optional
- Two medium tomatoes, chopped
- Four large eggs
- Chopped fresh cilantro
- Whole pita pieces of bread, toasted

Instructions:

1. In a large cast-iron or another heavy skillet, heat oil over medium heat. Add onion; cook and stir until tender, 4-6 minutes. Add garlic, seasonings, and, if desired, chilli sauce; cook 30 seconds longer. Add tomatoes; cook until mixture is thickened, stirring occasionally, 3-5 minutes.
2. With the back of a spoon, make four wells in the vegetable mixture; break an egg into each well. Cook, covered until egg whites are completely set and yolks begin to thicken but are not hard, 4-6 minutes. Sprinkle with cilantro; serve with pita bread.

Nutrition Per Serving: 159 calories,12g fat,186mg cholesterol,381mg sodium,7g protein.

Hoisin Turkey Lettuce Wraps

Preparation time: 10 minutes Cooking time: 15 minutes Servings: 4

Ingredients:

1. 1-pound lean ground turkey
2. 1/2 pound sliced fresh mushrooms
3. One medium sweet red pepper, diced
4. One medium onion, finely chopped
5. One medium carrot, shredded
6. One tablespoon sesame oil
7. 1/4 cup hoisin sauce
8. Two tablespoons balsamic vinegar
9. Two tablespoons reduced-sodium soy sauce
10. One tablespoon minced fresh ginger root
11. Two garlic cloves, minced
12. 8 Bibb or Boston lettuce leaves

Instructions:

1. In a large skillet, cook and crumble turkey with vegetables in sesame oil over medium-high heat until turkey is no longer pink, 8-10 minutes, breaking up turkey into crumbles. Stir in hoisin sauce, vinegar, soy sauce, ginger, and garlic; cook and stir over medium heat until sauce is slightly thickened about 5 minutes. Serve in lettuce leaves.

Nutrition Per Serving: 292 calories,13g fat,79mg cholesterol,629mg sodium,26g protein.

Aubergine & Olive Feast

Preparation time: 5 minutes Cooking time: 15 minutes Servings: 4

Ingredients:

- 10 oz halloumi (cut into slices).
- 1 aubergine (cut into bite size pieces).
- 3 oz butter.
- Twelve olives (pitted).
- 1 tsp paprika.
- 1 tsp chilli flakes.

Instructions:

2. Melt the butter in a large frying pan.
3. Place the aubergine chunks and olives in one half and halloumi in the other.
4. Season with paprika and chilli; cook for 8-10 minutes, occasionally turning to ensure halloumi is golden brown on both sides and aubergine is cooked through.

Nutrition Per Serving: Fat: 77g, Carbohydrates: 9g, Protein: 33g, Calories: 849

Keto Chilli-Con-Carne

Preparation time: 5 minutes Cooking time: 15 minutes Servings: 4

Ingredients:

- 16 oz minced beef (frozen & defrosted).
- 1 ½ cups canned chopped tomatoes.
- 3 oz cheddar cheese (grated).
- Two garlic cloves (crushed).
- One red onion (diced).
- ½ red pepper (diced).
- ½ yellow pepper (diced).
- 2 tsp tomato puree.
- 2 tsp coriander.
- 1 tsp chilli powder.

Instructions:

1. Preheat the oven at 180 degrees.
2. In a large frying pan, fry the onions and garlic cloves until tender. Stir in the beef and fry until browned and cooked through.
3. Add chopped tomatoes, red and yellow peppers, tomato puree, coriander, and chilli powder; fry 6-7 minutes until bubbling.
4. Pour into an ovenproof dish and sprinkle cheese on top.

5. Bake for 25-30 minutes.

Nutrition Per Serving: Fat: 40g, Carbohydrates: 7g, Protein: 31g, Calories: 529

Brats with Mustard Sauce

Preparation time: 10 minutes Cooking time: 25 minutes Servings: 4

Ingredients

- 1/3 cup half-and-half cream
- Two tablespoons stone-ground mustard
- 1/2 teaspoon dried minced onion
- 1/4 teaspoon pepper
- Dash paprika
- Four fully cooked bratwurst links (about 12 ounces)
- One can (14 ounces) sauerkraut, rinsed and drained, warmed

Instructions:

1. For the sauce, mix the first five ingredients. Cut each bratwurst into thirds; thread onto four metal or soaked wooden skewers.
2. Grill brats, covered, over medium heat until golden brown and heated through, 7-10 minutes, turning occasionally. Serve with sauerkraut and sauce.

Nutrition Per Serving: 341 calories, 28g fat, 73mg cholesterol, 1539mg sodium, 14g protein.

Moroccan Cauliflower and Almond Soup

Preparation time: 5=10 minutes Cooking time: 20 minutes Servings: 4

Ingredients

- One large head cauliflower (about 3-1/2 pounds), broken into florets
- 6 cups vegetable stock
- 3/4 cup sliced almonds, toasted and divided
- 1/2 cup plus two tablespoons minced fresh cilantro, divided
- Two tablespoons olive oil
- 1 to 3 teaspoons harissa chilli paste or hot pepper sauce
- 1/2 teaspoon ground cinnamon
- 1/2 teaspoon ground cumin
- 1/2 teaspoon ground coriander
- 1-1/4 teaspoons salt
- 1/2 teaspoon pepper

- Additional harissa chilli paste, optional

Instructions:

1. In a 5- or 6-qt. Slow cooker, combine cauliflower, vegetable stock, 1/2 cup almonds, 1/2 cup cilantro, and the next seven ingredients. Cook, covered, on low until cauliflower is tender, 6-8 hours.
2. Puree soup using an immersion blender. Or cool slightly and puree the soup in batches in a blender; return to slow cooker and heat through. Serve with remaining almonds and cilantro and, if desired, additional harissa.

Nutrition Per Serving: 116 calories, 8g fat, 0 cholesterol, 835mg sodium, 9g carbohydrate, 4g protein.

Mozzarella Pockets of Pleasure

Preparation time: 5 minutes Cooking time: 25 minutes Servings: 3

Ingredients:

- 3 eggs.
- 8 oz mozzarella (grated).
- 4 oz bacon (grilled).
- 2 oz cream cheese.
- ⅔ cup almond flour.
- ½ cup cheddar cheese (grated).
- ⅓ cup coconut flour.
- 2 tsp baking powder.
- 1 tsp salt.

Instructions:

1. Preheat oven at 350 degrees.
2. Microwave the cream cheese and mozzarella for 60 seconds. Stir and microwave for an additional 60 seconds.
3. Put one egg, almond flour, coconut flour, baking powder, and salt into a blender and pour in the melted cheese mixture. Blend until a dough forms.
4. Split the dough into eight pieces. Flatten each piece to form a 5-inch circle, place on a baking tray lined with baking paper.
5. Scramble the remaining two eggs and divide between each circle; do the same with bacon and cheddar cheese.
6. Fold the edges in and seal the semi-circle using fingertips.
7. Bake for 20 minutes or until lightly browned.

Nutrition Per Serving: Fat:18g, Carbohydrates: 6.5g, Protein: 16g, Calories: 258

What Waffle!

Preparation time: 5 minutes Cooking time: 15 minutes Servings: 4

Ingredients:

- 2 large eggs.
- 2 cups almond flour.
- 1 ½ cups almond milk (warm).
- ⅓ cup butter (melted).
- 2 tbsp erythritol.
- 4 tsp baking powder.
- 1 tsp vanilla extract.
- 1 tsp salt.

Instructions:

1. Mix baking powder, salt, and almond flour until well combined.
2. In a separate bowl, whisk the eggs until well combined.
3. Take the lukewarm almond milk and mix with the eggs, adding melted butter, erythritol, and vanilla extract.
4. Stir the egg mixture into the flour mixture until a dough is formed. Let sit for several minutes.
5. Cook in a hot waffle iron for 6-8 minutes.

Nutrition Per Serving: Fat: 31g, Carbohydrates: 8g, Protein: 11g, Calories: 345

Pseudo-Chile Rellenos Casserole

Preparation time: 10 minutes Cooking time: 15 minutes Servings: 4

Ingredients:

- 1/2 lb. ground or shredded meat
- 1/4 onion (chopped)
- 1 10 oz. can whole green chillies
- 1 1/2 cups cheddar cheese
- Two eggs
- 3/4 C milk
- 1/8 C flour
- 1 tsp cumin
- 1/2 tsp salt
- 1/2 tsp pepper
- Preheat oven to 375F

Instructions:

1. Cook hamburger meat and onion. (Option - cook chicken then shred it while cooking chopped onion) Drain, then add cumin, salt, and pepper.
2. Grease pan (I use 11x7 Pyrex)
3. Line the bottom of your pan with whole green chillies (chop extra green chillies for later).

4. Layer meat over green chillies. Top with cheese and chopped green chillies. Whisk together eggs and milk, then add flour and mix well. Pour this mixture over the dish. Bake for 35 to 40 minutes.
5. Two roasted fresh green chillies can be used instead of canned chillies

Nutrition Per Serving: Fat 160.3G, Protein: 105.3G, Net Carbs: 24.5G, Total Calories: 1979.9G

Keto Bacon Wrapped Shrimp

Preparation time: 5 minutes Cooking time: 15 minutes Servings: 3

Ingredients:

- 1 lb (450g) extra-large raw shrimp - peeled, deveined, tail on
- sea salt and pepper - to taste
- 1/4 tsp chilli powder
- 1/4 tsp cayenne pepper
- 1 tsp smoked paprika
- 1 Tbsp fresh lemon juice
- 1 Tbsp olive oil

- 6-8 very thin slices of bacon - (about 12 oz. / 340g)
- Keto white Sauce:
- 1 cup mayonnaise
- 1 Tbsp dijon mustard
- 2 tsp prepared horseradish
- 2 Tbsp apple cider vinegar
- 1 tsp garlic powder
- sea salt and pepper - to taste

Instructions:

1. Preheat the oven to 400°F (200°C) and line a large baking tray with parchment paper.
2. Place the raw shrimp into a bowl and sprinkle with seasonings. Drizzle olive oil and fresh lemon juice and gently toss to coat.
3. Cut the bacon strips in half and wrap each shrimp in one bacon half-slice. Insert a toothpick through the bacon to secure the wrap.
4. Arrange the shrimp in a single layer on the prepared pan. Roast the bacon-wrapped shrimp for 10-12 minutes, flipping it halfway.
5. Meanwhile, combine all sauce ingredients in a jug and whisk to emulsify. Refrigerate until ready to use.
6. Once the shrimp is done, carefully remove the toothpicks and transfer it to a serving plate.
7. Serve with white Keto sauce and Enjoy!

Nutrition Per Serving: Fat 81g, Saturated Fat 19g, Sodium 1857mg, Potassium 291mg, Carbohydrates 3g, Sugar 1g, Protein 35g

Baked Jalapeno Poppers

Preparation time: 10 minutes Cooking time: 20 minutes Servings: 6

Ingredients:

- 12 large jalapeños
- 12 oz. (340g) cream cheese - room temp
- 8 oz. (225g) shredded cheddar cheese
- 8 oz. (225g) bacon - cooked and crumbled
- 2-3 tbsp chopped chives
- 1/2 tsp garlic powder
- Sea salt and pepper - to taste

Instructions:

1. Preheat the oven to 360°F/180°C and line a large rimmed baking sheet* with parchment paper*.
2. Prepare the jalapeños: using a paring knife, cut each one in half, lengthwise. Carefully cut the ribs, then deseed and discard. Place the jalapeño halves on the prepared baking tray, cut side up.
3. In a mixing bowl*, add cream cheese, shredded cheese, crumbled bacon, chives, garlic powder, and season with salt and pepper to your taste. Mix until well combined.
4. Stuff each jalapeño with the cheese mixture, then place the baking tray in the preheated oven.
5. Bake for 15-20 minutes or until the peppers are tender and golden on tops.
6. Sprinkle with chives if desired and enjoy while hot!

Nutrition Per Serving: Fat 47g, Saturated Fat 24g, Cholesterol 127mg, Sodium 668mg, Potassium 260mg, Carbohydrates 5g, Fiber 1g, Sugar 3g, Protein 18g

Bacon & Egg Pick-me-up

Preparation time: 5 minutes Cooking time: 15 minutes Servings: 4

Ingredients:
- 8 large eggs.
- 5 oz bacon (slices).
- A handful of cherry tomatoes (halved).

Instructions:
1. In a large frying pan, fry bacon rashers until crispy. Set aside, leaving bacon fat in the pan.

2. Crack the eggs into the frying pan and fry eggs to your preferred taste.
3. When eggs are nearly cooked, throw in the cherry tomatoes and fry until lightly browned.

Nutrition Per Serving: Fat: 24g, Carbohydrates: 1g, Protein: 17g, Calories: 274

No-Fuss Egg Medley Muffins

Preparation time: 5 minutes Cooking time: 20 minutes Servings: 4

Ingredients:

- 12 large eggs.
- One onion (finely chopped).
- 6 oz cheddar cheese (grated).
- 5 oz bacon (cooked and diced).
- Pinch salt and pepper.

Instructions:

1. Preheat the oven at 175 degrees and grease a 12-hole muffin tray.
2. Equally, place onion and bacon to the bottom of each muffin tray hole.
3. In a large bowl, whisk the eggs, cheese, salt, and pepper.
4. Pour the egg mixture into each hole; on top of the onions and bacon.
5. Bake for 15-20 minutes, until browned and firm to the touch.

Nutrition Per Serving: Fat: 28g, Carbohydrates: 2g, Protein: 22g, Calories: 333

KETO BONUS RECIPES

Charming Cream Cheese Pancakes

Preparation time: 5 minutes Cooking time: 5 minutes Servings: 1

Ingredients:

- 2 large eggs
- 2 oz cream cheese.
- 1 tsp granulated sugar substitute.
- ½ tsp ground cinnamon.

Instructions:

1. Blend all ingredients until smooth. Allow resting for 2 minutes.
2. Grease a large frying pan and pour in ¼ of the mixture.
3. Cook for 2 minutes until golden, flip and cook for an additional minute.
4. Repeat the process until all mixture has gone.

Nutrition Per Serving: Fat: 30g, Carbohydrates: 3g, Protein: 16g, Calories: 346

Stay Right Soldiers & Egg

Preparation time: 5 minutes Cooking time: 10 minutes Servings: 1

Ingredients:
- 1 large egg.
- 2 oz cheddar cheese (cut in chunky wedges).

Instructions:
1. Gently place the egg in a lidded saucepan of cold water, bring to the boil.
2. When the water is boiling excessively, turn off the heat and remove the pan away from the heat.
3. To create a soft and runny centre, leave the egg sitting in hot water for 4 minutes.
4. Take the egg out of the water and crack off the top of the egg. Use the cheese sticks to dunk into the egg.

Nutrition Per Serving: Fat: 22g, Carbohydrates: 1g, Protein: 17g, Calories: 270

Bacon & Avocado Guacamole Sandwich

Preparation time: 5 minutes Cooking time: 15 minutes Servings: 1

Ingredients:
- 6 slices bacon.
- Two avocados.
- Two small onions (diced).
- 2 tbsp lime juice.
- 2 tbsp garlic powder.
- Cooking spray.

Instructions:
1. Preheat the oven at 180 degrees.
2. Spray a baking tray with cooking spray, cook the bacon 15-20 minutes until crispy.
3. Remove seeds from avocados; in a massive bowl, mash the avocado flesh with a fork.
4. Add onions, garlic, and lime juice; mash until well combined.
5. Allow the crispy bacon to cool and place one slice on a plate; top with 2 tbsp of avocado guacamole. Place another bacon slice on top and add another 2 tbsp of guacamole and top with bacon. Repeat to make another sandwich.

Nutrition Per Serving: Fat: 46g, Carbohydrates: 11g, Protein: 23g, Calories: 544

Cheesy Chicken Fritters

Preparation time: 5 minutes Cooking time: 20 minutes Servings: 3

Ingredients:

- 1.5 lb (700g) skinless, boneless chicken breast
- Two medium eggs
- 1/3 cup almond flour
- 1 cup shredded mozzarella cheese
- 2 Tbsp fresh basil - finely chopped
- 2 Tbsp chives - chopped
- 2 Tbsp parsley - chopped
- 1/2 tsp garlic powder
- a pinch of sea salt and new ground black pepper - or to taste
- 1 Tbps olive oil

Instructions:

1. Place the chicken breast on a chopping board and using a sharp knife, chop it into tiny pieces, then place them in a large mixing bowl.
2. Into the large bowl, stir in almond flour, eggs, mozzarella, basil, chives, parsley, garlic powder, salt, and pepper. Mix well to combine.
3. Heat oil in a large non-stick pan, over medium-low heat. With an ice cream scoop or a large spoon, scoop into the chicken mixture and transfer it to the pan, then slightly flatten to create a pancake. Don't overcrowd the pan, cook the pancakes in batches, about 4 per shipment.
4. Fry until golden brown on both sides, about 6-8 minutes. Keep in mind that you need to cook them at medium-low temp. Otherwise, they will burn on the outside but won't get well prepared on the inside.

Nutrition Per Serving: Fat 21g, Saturated Fat 6g, Cholesterol 212g, Sodium 405g, Protein 47g

Roasted Chicken with Carrots

Preparation time: 10 minutes Cooking time: 15 minutes Servings: 4

Ingredients:

- Four chicken thighs
- 1½ pounds carrots, peeled and trimmed
- One large onion, peeled and cut into eighths
- One head of garlic
- Four tablespoons olive oil
- One tablespoon chopped fresh rosemary
- Kosher salt and freshly ground black pepper, to taste

Instructions:

1. Preheat the oven to 425°F.
2. Arrange the carrots and onion in a single layer on a greased baking sheet.
3. Slice the top of a head of garlic; discard the top, and place it on the tray.

4. Drizzle 2 tablespoons of olive oil over the vegetables; season with the rosemary, and salt and pepper.
5. Top with the chicken thighs. Rub each leg with one teaspoon olive oil; season with salt and pepper.
6. Roast in the oven until the chicken skin is golden, and the carrots are tender, 15 to 20 minutes.
7. To serve, divide the vegetables and chicken thighs among four plates.

Nutrition Per Serving: Calories 553g, Fat 39g, Carbs 24g, Protein 37g, Sugars 10g

Crispy Keto Cauliflower Hash

Preparation time: 5 minutes Cooking time: 10 minutes Servings: 2

Ingredients:

- 2 large eggs.
- 12 oz cauliflower rice (frozen).
- Olive oil for frying.
- ½ cup parmesan (grated).
- ½ tsp salt.
- ¼ tsp black pepper.
- ⅛ tsp paprika.

Instructions:

1. Microwave the cauliflower rice and allow it to soften.
2. Mix all ingredients, except the eggs, together with the rice until well combined.
3. When the mixture is thoroughly combined, stir in the eggs and mix well.
4. Heat olive oil in a large frying pan and scoop 1 heaped tbsp of mixture into the pan. Fry for 2 minutes on each side until crispy and golden brown.
5. Repeat the process until all mixture has gone.

Nutrition Per Serving: Fat: 12g, Carbohydrates: 4g, Protein: 15g, Calories: 188g

Perfect Peanut Butter Breakfast Balls

Preparation time: 5 minutes Cooking time: 35 minutes Servings: 4

Ingredients:

- Two cups peanut butter (smooth).
- ¾ cup coconut flour.
- ½ cup monk fruit sweetened maple syrup.

Instructions:

1. Line a large baking tray with greaseproof paper.
2. In a large bowl, mix all ingredients until a thick batter is formed.
3. Mould the batter into small balls and place them on the baking tray.
4. Refrigerate 40-60 minutes until firm.

Nutrition Per Serving: Fat: 15g, Carbohydrates: 7g, Protein: 8g, Calories: 173

Tantalizing Tuna & Spinach Mix

Preparation time: 5 minutes Cooking time: 15 minutes Servings: 2

Ingredients:

- 4 large eggs.
- 10 oz tinned tuna (in olive oil).
- ½ cup mayonnaise.
- One avocado (sliced).
- One onion (finely diced).
- Salt and pepper (to season).

Instructions:

1. Bring a large pan of water to the boil and lower in the eggs. Cook for 8 minutes.
2. In a bowl, mix tuna, mayonnaise, onion, salt, and pepper.
3. Chop the hard-boiled eggs into halves and place them on a plate with avocado slices and spinach.
4. Place the tuna mixture on top of spinach.

Nutrition Per Serving: Fat: 79g, Carbohydrates: 3g, Protein: 53g, Calories: 952

Keto Filling Veg Soup

Preparation time: 5 minutes Cooking time: 20 minutes Servings: 10

Ingredients:

- 8 cups vegetable broth.
- Two tins tomatoes (chopped).
- Two bell peppers (diced).
- One large onion (diced).
- Four cloves garlic (crushed).
- One cauliflower (cut into florets).
- 2 tbsp olive oil.
- 1 tbsp Italian seasoning.

Instructions:

1. Heat olive oil in a large saucepan.
2. Saute onions and bell peppers for 10 minutes until tender and lightly browned; stir in garlic and cook for an additional minute.
3. Add the broth, cauliflower, tomatoes, and Italian seasoning; bring to the boil. Cover, reduce heat, and simmer for 15-20 minutes until the veg is tender.

Nutrition Per Serving: Fat: 13g, Carbohydrates: 3g, Protein: 9g, Calories: 83g

Smothered Garlic Butter Chicken

Preparation time: 5 minutes Cooking time: 15 minutes Servings: 4

Ingredients:

- 4 chicken breasts (defrosted).
- 6 oz butter (room temperature).
- One garlic clove (crushed).
- 3 tbsp olive oil.

- 1 tsp lemon juice.
- ½ tsp salt.
- ½ tsp garlic powder.

Instructions:

1. Mix butter, garlic powder, garlic clove, lemon juice, and salt. When well combined, set aside.
2. In a large frying pan, heat the oil and fry chicken breasts until thoroughly cooked through and golden brown.
3. Place chicken on a plate and smoothly smother each chicken breast with a garlic butter mixture.

Nutrition Per Serving: Fat: 72g, Carbohydrates: 2g, Protein: 62g, Calories: 899

Antipasto Salad Recipe

Preparation time: 10 minutes Cooking time: 5 minutes Servings: 4

Ingredients:

- One large head or two hearts romaine chopped
- 4 ounces prosciutto cut in strips
- 4 ounces salami or pepperoni cubed
- 1/2 cup artichoke hearts sliced
- 1/2 cup olives mix of black and green
- 1/2 cup hot or sweet peppers pickled or roasted
- Italian dressing to taste

Instructions:

1. Combine all ingredients in a large salad bowl. Toss with dressing.

Nutrition Per Serving: Calories: 462kcal, Carbohydrates: 7g, Protein: 14g, Fat: 41g, Fat: 11g

Turkey Basil-Mayo

Preparation time: 5 minutes Cooking time: 15 minutes Servings: 2

Ingredients:

- 1/2 cup gluten-free mayonnaise (I like Hellmann's Olive Oil Mayo)
- Six large basil leaves, torn
- One teaspoon lemon juice
- One garlic clove, chopped
- salt
- pepper

Instructions:

2. Combine ingredients in a small food processor then process until smooth. Alternatively, mince basil and garlic then whisk all ingredients together. It can be done a couple of days ahead of time.
3. Layout two large lettuce leaves, then layer on one slice of turkey and slather with Basil-Mayo. Layer on the second slice of turkey followed by the bacon and a few slices of both avocado and tomato. Season lightly with salt and pepper, then fold the bottom up, the sides in, and roll like a burrito. Slice in half then serves cold.

Nutrition Per Serving: Calories: 42kcal, Carbohydrates: 32g, Protein: 44g, Fat: 24g, Fat: 18g

Sesame Tofu with Eggplant

Preparation time: 5 minutes Cooking time: 15 minutes Servings: 4

Ingredients:

- 1-pound block firm tofu
- 1 cup (31g) chopped cilantro
- Three tablespoons rice vinegar
- Four tablespoons toasted sesame oil
- Two cloves garlic, finely minced
- One teaspoon crushed red pepper flakes

- Two teaspoons Swerve confectioners
- One whole (458 g) eggplant
- One tablespoon olive oil
- Salt and pepper to taste
- ¼ cup sesame seeds
- ¼ cup of soy sauce

Instructions:

1. Preheat oven to 200°F. Remove the block of tofu from its packaging and wrap it with some paper towels. Place a plate on top of it and weigh it down. I used a massive tin of vegetables in this picture, but you can use handy. Let the tofu sit for a while to press some of the water out.
2. Place about ¼ cup of cilantro, three tablespoons rice vinegar, two tablespoons toasted sesame oil, minced garlic, crushed red pepper flakes, and Swerve into a large mixing bowl. Whisk together.
3. Peel and julienne the eggplant. You can julienne roughly by hand as I did, or use a mandolin with a julienne attachment for more precise "noodles." Mix the eggplant with the marinade.

4. Add the tablespoon of olive oil to a skillet over medium-low heat. Eggplant until it softens. The eggplant will soak up all of the liquids, so if you have issues with it sticking to the pan, feel free to add a little bit more sesame or olive oil. Just be sure to adjust your nutrition tracking.
5. Turn the oven off. Stir the remaining cilantro into the eggplant then transfer the noodles to an oven-safe dish. Cover with a lid, or foil, and place into the oven to keep warm. Wipe out the skillet and return to the stovetop to heat up again.
6. Unwrap the tofu then cut into eight slices. Spread the sesame seeds on a plate. Press both sides of each piece of tofu into the seeds.
7. Add two tablespoons of sesame oil to the skillet. Fry both sides of the tofu for 5 minutes each, or until they start to crisp up. Pour the ¼ cup of soy sauce into the pan and coat the pieces of tofu. Cook until the tofu slices look browned and caramelized with the soy sauce.
8. Remove the noodles from the oven and plate the tofu on top.

Nutrition Per Serving: 292.75 Calories, 24.45g Fats, 6.87g Net Carbs

Creamy Coconut Keto Chicken Curry

Preparation time: 5 minutes Cooking time: 20 minutes Servings: 4

Ingredients:
- 24 oz chicken thighs (lean & defrosted).
- One ¼ cup of coconut milk.
- ⅓ cup red onion (diced).
- 4 tsp curry paste.
- Cooking spray.

Instructions:
1. Preheat the oven at 200 degrees.
2. Rub chicken with 2 tsp of curry paste. Set aside for 15-20 minutes.
3. Spray a large frying pan with cooking spray, fry onions and add in remaining 2 tsp curry paste and fry 3-4 minutes.
4. Place chicken thighs in the pan with onions and sear for 3-4 minutes. Turn the chicken over, reduce heat, and pour in coconut milk. Simmer for 7-8 minutes.
5. Pour the curry mixture into a large ovenproof dish and bake for 15-20 minutes.

Nutrition Per Serving: Fat: 27g, Carbohydrates: 2g, Protein: 34g, Calories: 374

Beautiful Broccoli Cheese Baked Bites

Preparation time: 10 minutes Cooking time: 25 minutes Servings: 4

Ingredients:

- 2 cups broccoli (florets).
- Two eggs.
- One cup cheddar cheese (grated).
- ½ cup spinach.
- ¼ cup onions (diced).
- ¼ cup parmesan (grated).
- ⅓ cup sour cream.
- One lemon zest.

Instructions:

1. Preheat the oven at 180 degrees.
2. Place broccoli in a microwave-safe bowl with ¼ cup of water. Microwave for 3 minutes on high or until broccoli is tender.
3. Chop broccoli florets into small pieces and place in a large bowl. Add all other ingredients and mix well until thoroughly combined.
4. Line an ovenproof dish with greaseproof paper and pour in the mixture.
5. Bake for 20-25 minutes until puffed and browned.
6. Cool for 10 minutes and cut into 24 square bites.

Nutrition Per Serving: Fat: 6g, Carbohydrates: 1g, Protein: 6g, Calories: 61

Keto flat bread

Preparation time: 5 minutes Cooking time: 15 minutes Servings: 8

Ingredients:

For the Crust:

- 2 cups half-and-half grated mozzarella cheese
- 2 tbsp. Cream cheese
- ¾ cup almond flour
- ½ tsp. Sea salt
- ⅛ tsp. Dried thyme

For the Topping:

- 1 cup grated Mexican cheese
- ½ red onion, small and sliced
- 4 oz. Low carbohydrate sliced ham,
- ¼ medium apple, unpeeled and sliced
- ⅛ tsp. Thyme, dried Salt and pepper

Instructions:

1. Fill a saucepan with a little water and bring to the boil, then turn the heat to low. Place the saucepan inside a metal mixing bowl to form a double boiler, and add the mozzarella cheese, cream cheese, almond flour, thyme and salt. Stir with a spatula.
2. Cook until the cheese melts, and mix the ingredients into a dough. Pour some onto a 12-inch pizza tray covered with parchment paper. Roll the dough into a ball and place onto the center of the parchment paper. Pat into a disc shape to cover the pan.
3. Place the dough and the parchment paper on the pizza pan, poking holes throughout the dough with a fork, and bake for 6-8 minutes at 425°F. Remove.
4. Spread the toppings over the flatbread, along with the cheese, onion, apple and the ham. Cover with more cheese. Season with thyme, salt and pepper.
5. Bake again at 350°F for 5-7 minutes. Remove once the cheese begins to brown. Let cool before slicing.

Nutrition Per Serving: Calories: 257 Fat: 22g Net Carbs: 5g Protein: 18g

Zucchini boats

Preparation time: 5 minutes Cooking time: 15 minutes Servings: 1

Ingredients:

- 2 large zucchini
- 2 tbsp. Butter
- 3 oz. Shredded cheddar cheese
- 1 cup broccoli
- 6 oz. Shredded rotisserie chicken
- 1 stalk green onion
- 2 tbsp. Sour cream Salt and pepper

Directions

1. Cut the zucchini in half lengthwise, scooping out the core until you are left with a boat shape.
2. Into each zucchini pour a little melted butter, season and place into the oven at 400°F, baking for about 18 minutes.
3. In a bowl, combine the chicken, broccoli and sour cream.
4. Place the chicken mixture inside the hollowed zucchinis.
5. Top with cheddar cheese and bake for an additional 10-15 minutes.

Nutrition Per Serving: Calories: 480, Fat: 35g Net Carbs: 5g Protein: 28g

Keto stromboli

Preparation time: 5 minutes Cooking time: 15 minutes Servings: 4

Ingredients:

- 1¼ cup shredded mozzarella cheese
- 4 tbsp. Almond flour
- 3 tbsp. Coconut flour
- 1 egg
- 1 tsp. Italian seasoning
- 4 oz. Ham
- 4 oz. Cheddar cheese Salt and pepper

Directions

1. Melt the mozzarella cheese in the microwave for about 1 minute, stirring occasionally so as not to burn it.
2. In a separate bowl, mix almond flour, coconut flour, salt, and pepper and add the melted mozzarella cheese. Mix well. Then, after letting it cool down a bit, add the eggs and combine again.
3. Place the mixture on parchment paper, laying a second layer on top. Using your hands or rolling pin, flatten it out into a rectangle.
4. Remove the top layer of paper and with a knife cut diagonal lines toward the middle of the dough. They should be cut ⅓ of the way in on one side. Then, cut diagonal lines on the other side too.
5. On the top of the dough, alternate slices of ham and cheese. Then, fold one side over, and then the other, to cover the filling.
6. Place on a baking sheet and bake at 400°F for 15-20 minutes.

Nutrition Per Serving: Calories: 305, Fat: 22g Net Carbs: 5g Protein: 25g

Keto chicken sandwich

Preparation time: 5 minutes Cooking time: 15 minutes Servings: 2

Ingredients:

For the Bread:

- 3 eggs
- 3 oz. Cream cheese

- ⅛ tsp. Cream of tartar Salt Garlic powder

For the Filling:

- 1 tbsp. Mayonnaise
- 1 tsp. Sriracha
- 2 slices bacon
- 3 oz. Chicken
- 2 slices pepper jack cheese
- 2 grape tomatoes
- ¼ avocado

Directions

1. Separate the eggs in different bowls. In the egg whites add cream tartar, salt and beat until stiff peaks form.
2. In another bowl, beat the egg yolks with cream cheese. Incorporate the mixture into the egg white mixture and combine carefully.
3. Place the batter on a parchment paper and form little square shapes that look like bread slices. Sparkle garlic powder on top and bake at 300°F for 25 minutes.
4. While the bread is baking, cook the chicken and bacon in a frying pan, seasoning to taste.
5. When the bread is done, remove from oven and let cool for 10-15 minutes. Then, make the sandwich with the cooked chicken and bacon, adding the mayo, sriracha, tomatoes, cheese and mashed avocado to taste.

Nutrition Per Serving: Calories: 360, Fat: 28g, Net Carbs: 3g, Protein: 22g

Tuna bites with avocado

Preparation time: 5 minutes Cooking time: 15 minutes Servings: 8

Ingredients:

- 10 oz. Drained canned tuna
- ¼ cup mayo 1 avocado
- ¼ cup parmesan cheese
- ⅓ cup almond flour
- ½ tsp. Garlic powder
- ¼ tsp. Onion powder
- ½ cup coconut oil Salt and pepper

Directions

1. In a bowl mix all the ingredients (except coconut oil). Form little balls and cover with almond flour.

2. Fry them in a pan medium heat with melted coconut oil (it has to be hot) until they seem browned on all sides.

Nutrition Per Serving: Calories: 137, Fat: 12g Net Carbs: 10g Protein: 6g

Keto green salad

Preparation time: 5 minutes Cooking time: 15 minutes Servings: 1

Ingredients:

- 2 oz. Mixed greens
- 3 tbsp. Roasted pine nuts
- 2 tbsp. Raspberry vinaigrette
- 2 tbsp. Parmesan, shaved
- 2 slices bacon Salt and pepper

Directions

1. Cook the bacon in a pan until crunchy and well browned. Break up into pieces, and add to the rest of the ingredients in a bowl.
2. Dress the salad with the raspberry vinaigrette.

Nutrition Per Serving: Calories: 480Fat: 37g Net Carbs: 4g Protein: 17g

keto stuffed hot dogs

Preparation time: 5 minutes Cooking time: 15 minutes Servings: 6

Ingredients:

- 6 hot dogs
- 12 slices bacon
- 2 oz. Cheddar
- ½ tsp. Cheese garlic powder
- ½ tsp. Onion powder Salt and pepper

Directions

1. Make a little slit in each hot dog, and stuff them with slices of cheese. Wrap each hot dog with 2 slices of overlapping bacon, and secure with toothpicks.

2. On top of a wire rack (with a cookie sheet below), place the hotdogs. Season them and bake at 400°F for 20-25 minutes approx.

Nutrition Per Serving: Calories: 385, Fat: 34g Net Carbs: 0.5g Protein: 17g

Easy egg soup

Preparation time: 5 minutes Cooking time: 15 minutes Servings: 1

Ingredients:

- 1½ cups chicken broth
- ½ cube of chicken bouillon
- 1 tbsp. Bacon fat
- 2 eggs
- 1 tsp. Chili garlic paste

Directions

1. In a pan on the stove on a medium-high heat, add the chicken broth, bouillon cube and bacon fat. Bring into boil and incorporate chili garlic paste and mix.
2. Whisk the eggs and add them to the chicken while stirring, then let sit for a few minutes.

Nutrition Per Serving: Calories: 280, Fat: 25g, Net Carbs: 2.7g, Protein: 13g

Original nasi lemak

Preparation time: 5 minutes Cooking time: 15 minutes Servings: 2

Ingredients:

For the Chicken & Egg:

- 2 chicken thighs, boneless
- ½ tsp. Curry powder
- ¼ tsp. Turmeric powder
- ½ tsp. Lime juice

- ½ tbsp. Coconut oil
- 1 egg
- A pinch of salt

For the Nasi Lemak:

- 3 tbsp. Coconut milk
- 3 slices ginger
- ½ small shallot
- 1 cup riced cauliflower
- 4 slices cucumber
- Salt

Directions

1. Rice the cauliflower and strain the water.
2. Prepare the curry powder, turmeric powder, lemon juice and salt, and marinate the chicken thighs for an hour or two in the fridge. Remove and fry.
3. Boil the coconut milk, ginger and shallot in a saucepan. When it bubbles, incorporate the cauliflower rice and mix.
4. Serve with the marinated fried chicken and fried egg.

Nutrition Per Serving: Calories: 502, Fat: 40g, Net Carbs: 7g, Protein: 28g,

Keto sausage and pepper soup

Preparation time: 5 minutes Cooking time: 15 minutes Servings: 6

Ingredients:

- 30 oz. Pork sausage
- 1 tbsp. Olive oil
- 10 oz. Raw spinach
- 1 medium green bell pepper
- 1 can tomatoes with jalapeños
- 4 cups beef stock
- 1 tbsp. Onion powder
- 1 tbsp. Chili powder
- 1 tsp. Cumin garlic powder
- 1 tsp. Italian seasoning Salt

Directions

1. In a large pot, heat the olive oil over a medium heat until hot and cook the sausage. Stir.
2. Chop the green pepper and add to the pot. Stir well. Season with salt and pepper. Add the tomatoes and jalapeños. Stir.
3. Add the spinach on top and cover the pot. When it is wilted, incorporate spices and broth and combine.
4. Cover the pot again and let cook for about 30 minutes (heat medium-low). When it is done, remove the lid and let the soup simmer for around 10 minutes.

Nutrition Per Serving: Calories: 525, Fat: 45g, Net Carbs: 4g, Protein: 28g

Fresh Keto Sandwich

Preparation time: 5 minutes Cooking time: 15 minutes Servings: 1

Ingredients:

Cucumber
½ oz. Boursin cheese Meat of your choice, sliced

Directions

1. Slice the cucumber in half and scoop out the core and seeds with a spoon. Remove the hard-outer skin carefully with a knife.
2. In one side place cheese. In the other side fold meat. Place together to form a sandwich!

Nutrition Per Serving: Calories: 195, Fat: 14g, Net Carbs: 8g, Protein: 18g

Original squash lasagna

Preparation time: 5 minutes Cooking time: 15 minutes Servings: 12

Ingredients:

- 1 lb. Spaghetti squash
- 3 lb. Ground beef
- 30 slices mozzarella cheese
- 1 large jar marinara sauce
- 32 oz. Whole milk ricotta cheese

Directions

- Cut the spaghetti squash in two halves, placing them face down onto a baking dish. Add a half inch or so of water. Bake for 45 minutes. When finished, carefully pull out the meat of the squash.
- In a frying pan, cook the ground beef the meat in a pan and add marinara sauce.
- In a greased baking pan, place a layer of spaghetti squash, cover with the meat sauce, mozzarella and ricotta. Repeat until the pan is full.
- Bake for 35 minutes at 375°F.

Nutrition Per Serving: Calories: 710, Fat: 60g, Net Carbs: 17g, Protein: 45g

Keto Chili soup

Preparation time: 5 minutes Cooking time: 15 minutes Servings: 4

Ingredients:

- 2 tbsp. Butter, unsalted
- 2 onions
- 1 pepper
- 8 chicken thighs (boneless)
- 8 slices of bacon
- 1 tsp. Thyme
- 1 tsp. Salt
- 1 tsp. Pepper
- 1 tbsp. Garlic, minced
- 1 tbsp. Coconut flour
- 3 tbsp. Lemon juice
- 1 cup chicken stock
- ¼ cup unsweetened coconut milk
- 3 tbsp. Tomato paste

DIRECTIONS

1. Place the butter in the center of the crockpot.
2. Slice the onion and pepper, and add to the crockpot. Then add the chicken thighs. Top with the bacon slices.
3. Season with salt, pepper, minced garlic, and coconut flour. Add the lemon juice, chicken stocks, coconut milk and tomato paste.
4. Cook on low for 6 hours. When it is done, stir and serve.

Nutrition Per Serving: Calories: 395, Fat: 20g, Net Carbs: 8g, Protein: 40g

Chicken nuggets for keto nuts

Preparation time: 5 minutes Cooking time: 15 minutes Servings: 4

Ingredients:

- 1 chicken breast, precooked
- ½ ounce grated parmesan
- 2 tbsp. Almond flour
- ½ tsp. Baking powder
- 1 egg
- 1 tbsp. Water

Directions

1. Cut the chicken breast into slices and then into bite size pieces. Set aside.

2. Combine the parmesan, almond flour, baking powder, and water. Stir.
3. Cover the chicken pieces into the batter, and then place directly into the hot oil. Remove when golden.

Nutrition Per Serving: Calories: 165, Fat: 9g, Net Carbs: 3g, Protein: 25g

CONCLUSION:

One of the main keys to any successful diet or lifestyle change has always been the recipes that fit in with the principles of the diet. I am sure there are many ways to achieve ketosis, and to attain that weight loss goal. However, you definitely do not want to get there by just having the same old dishes over and over again.

Variety is the name of the game here, which is crucial in ensuring the sustainability of the ketogenic diet. With the flavorful and delicious recipes found in this step by step keto cookbook, they will be useful additions for any keto dieter at any stage of their ketogenic journey. I have yet to see anyone complain about having too many easy yet delicious recipes!

For the beginners who have gotten this recipe cookbook, it would be quite useful for you to take the 28-day meal plan as a helpful guide, but you should definitely step out from that comfort zone sooner or later as you progress along your keto adventure! This is what the multiple recipes are for, so that you can pick and choose those which are most attractive to your palate.

ONE LAST THING...

If you enjoyed this book or found it useful, I'd be very grateful if you'd post a short review on Amazon. Your support really does make a difference and I read all the reviews personally so I can get your feedback and make this book even better.

Thanks again for your support!

Printed in Great Britain
by Amazon

77960749R00061